UNDERWATER
GUIDE TO

Coral Fishes

OF THE INDIAN OCEAN

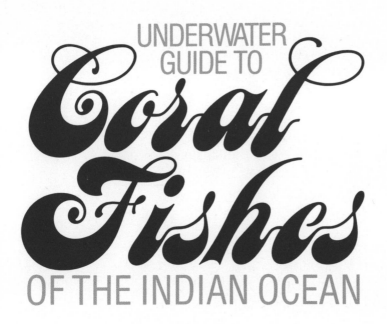

UNDERWATER GUIDE TO
Coral Fishes
OF THE INDIAN OCEAN

Brent Addison and Jeremy Tindall

SOUTHERN
BOOK PUBLISHERS

To our wives Liz and Rachel for their patience while we obtained the photographs, and their assistance with editing

My soul is full of longing
For the secret of the sea
and the heart of the great ocean
sends a thrilling pulse through me
                              Longfellow

ISBN 1 86812 282 4

First edition, first impression 1990

Published by
Southern Book Publishers (Pty) Ltd
P.O. Box 3103, Halfway House 1685

Cover design by Michael Barnett
Set in 10 on 12 pt Hanover
by Unifoto, Cape Town
Printed and bound by CTP Book Printers, Cape
BK1926

FOREWORD

Every now and again — but not all that often — you meet people who have the ability to combine their intellectual and sporting interests not only for their own enjoyment, but for passing on something worthwhile to others.

Diving is a demanding sport in which not everyone can participate. Yet the underwater realm is breathtakingly beautiful and, if made accessible through the medium of photography, can bring joy and wonder to thousands of people not capable of venturing below the surface of the sea themselves.

This book is aimed at precisely this need. It is not a scientific treaty, but it reflects the beauty, the thrill and the joy experienced by divers in the clear water among reefs with their myriads of fish, corals and other organisms. Most of the photographs were taken off the Zululand coast on the southern extremities of the Indian Ocean's coral-bearing reefs. From many years of diving experience I know that their beauty compares with the best in the world.

The photographers — Brent Addison and his friend, Jerry Tindall — belong to that rare breed of people who can, and really are, transmitting the joy of their own diving to others.

This book, I am sure, will be a source of pleasure to many, many people. It may inspire some to venture underwater themselves. Others will be content just to gaze at the photographs and thus to also experience this part of God's creation through the lens of the underwater camera.

It is appropriate that I thank these divers for the service they have thus rendered and to wish them every success in their future activities below the waves of the oceans of the world.

Dr Allan Heydorn
Director: Southern African Nature Foundation

CONTENTS

INTRODUCTION

Given the present rise in public awareness of natural history and nature conservation, it is surprising that few people recognise the sea as the largest "reserve" in the world. The oceans of the world cover some 70% of the earth's surface and host an entirely fascinating and largely unexplored world. Most of us humans do not know or appreciate the life that exists beneath the waves. However, more and more people are taking up the sports of snorkelling or scuba diving. Anyone who dons a mask and looks under the water will be amazed at what can be seen but will not easily be able to identify the fish. This is what this book is all about: it is a guide for easy identification of some of the fish one is likely to see in the coral areas off the South African coast.

Most of the fish in this book will be found not only off our coast but in the entire Indo-Pacific region so that the visitor to Mauritius or the Seychelles will also find this book useful.

There are more than 2 000 species of marine fish found in the waters covered by this guide. However, the descriptions in this book are limited to only 110. For species not covered the reader is referred to *Smiths' Sea Fishes*.

This book is not intended in any way to be a scientific work and as such, technical details as to the structure of the fish or the number of gill rakers are not given. The purist should use *Smiths' Sea Fishes*, a comprehensive work, which we found invaluable in preparing this book. We have concentrated on descriptions of the fish and the most likely places where they will be seen, in order to provide a "field guide" with the prime purpose of fish identification. For example, many of the fish seen are not found swimming on the top of a reef but near the surface of the water; some fish are solitary, others are seen in groups; some fish are nocturnal and difficult to find during the day. This is the kind of information provided here.

Of particular importance is that all the photographs appearing in this book were taken underwater and hence the colours are accurate: most fish when removed from the water immediately lose their beautiful colours. The photographs here not only show the true colours but in many cases the habitat and surroundings in which the fish are normally found. The world underwater is truly fascinating and we hope this book will excite the reader to explore it further.

NOTES ON THE SPECIES DESCRIPTIONS

All South African fish have been allocated numbers by the JLB Smith Institute of Ichthyology. The fish appearing in this book are in Smiths' number sequence, this number appearing in brackets after the scientific name.

The scientific names are taken from *Smiths' Sea Fishes*, as are most of the English and Afrikaans common names, and should a fish have other common names either in South Africa or elsewhere these are also given. A few fish appearing in this book are not common to South African waters. However, as this book is intended to be used not only in South Africa itself, they have been included. Fish that are nocturnal are referred to as rare. *Smiths' Sea Fishes* is the ultimate authority on sea fishes off the South African coast and is recommended for readers who require further information.

For each fish, its size, a description, its common habitat, its feeding habits and some general information are given. Most of the general comments are based on observations or experiences of the authors themselves. The sizes in all cases, except for the rays, reflect the maximum length of the fish. Sizes for rays are given as the maximum width of the disc, which is felt to be more relevant.

When identifying fish particular note should be taken of the size and shape of the fish, in addition to noting the various colours and patterns. Each family of fish has a distinctive body shape and this will assist greatly in making identifications. For example, all butterflyfish are compressed and have rounded, almost disc-shaped, bodies. Rockcod are more elongated and do not have compressed bodies. Many of the fish that the reader will see may not have their fins extended and this should be remembered when identifying them. A good example is the sailfin tang, which has a beautiful dorsal fin when extended as shown in the photograph of it in this book.

Many fish display extreme colour variations depending on growth, their sex, the time of day, whether they are being cleaned by cleaner wrasse, and differences within the same species. Where possible we have either provided photographs of the differences or described them.

The fish appearing in the book are commonly found in and around coral reefs, which on our east coast extend from St Lucia northwards. We have not attempted to discuss exact distributions; they are ably described in both *Smiths' Sea Fishes* and Rudy van der Elst's book *A Guide to the Common Sea Fishes of Southern Africa*.

REEFS OFF THE SOUTH AFRICAN EAST COAST

No book on sea fishes found off the south-east coast of Africa would be complete without some description of popular and accessible diving areas. A complete coverage would be beyond the scope of this book, so only a few of the most popular reefs are described, particularly those that provide good photographic opportunities.

SODWANA AREA

Sodwana Bay is a very attractive area of the northern Natal coast. It is run by the Natal Parks Board and is one of the most popular fishing and diving spots in South Africa. There are some 600 well shaded camping sites with excellent ablution facilities. Special areas have been demarcated for cleaning fish and for compressors to fill diving tanks. Wood for camp fires can be purchased, ice is available and it is possible to rent a freezer if required. There is a well stocked shop carrying food, fishing tackle and almost anything else that may be required. Petrol is available in the camp itself and recently a garage and workshop have been established a few kilometres from the gate. There are several excellent diving venues all reached through the Sodwana Bay reserve, or Jesser Point as it is named on most maps. The reserve itself extends 2 km south and 9 km north of Jesser Point. The bay provides sufficient protection to allow easy launching of boats although there are times when high seas prohibit this. Almost all diving in the Sodwana area is done from a boat. Some of the reefs in this area are named for their distance from Jesser Point; none for their distance from the shore.

Jesser Point

Off Jesser Point, which covers the south side of Sodwana, is a reef that continues out from the rocks at the beach. These rocks are exposed at low tide. The reef is elbow shaped, angling out to sea past the rock the ski-boaters call the pulpit, and then heading in a northerly direction for several hundred metres. At low tide and with large swells this reef can be quite dangerous and very stirred up. However, on a calm day the reef is easy to swim out to from the shore. When diving here care must be taken as the ski-boats leaving the bay travel directly over this reef.

Two Mile Reef

This is possibly the most popular diving reef in South Africa. As the name suggests it is some 3 km (2 miles) north of Jesser Point. The reef, about 4 km long and more than 1 km wide, has in recent years been marked by buoys to which dive boats can be attached. These buoys have been placed at the best dive sites on the reef although those who know the area well talk about the interesting places further north and on the outer perimeter of the reef. The shallow parts of Two Mile are less than 10 m deep while on the outer edges depths of 30 m can be found.

For the underwater photographer this reef is a paradise. Each coral head hosts hundreds of different coral fish, large shoals of bait fish and a variety of larger reef fish. In addition game fish can be seen drifting past in the mid-water. Large potato bass and moray eels are common and make excellent photographic subjects.

Two Mile is a safe diving reef but two points should be noted. Firstly, in the summer months there is frequently a strong current which can flow at a rate of up to 4 knots. It generally flows from north to south but can occasionally flow in the opposite direction in the shallower areas. Secondly, large swells can be encountered which cause severe surges underwater. These surges can throw a diver around and will almost certainly stir up the sediment, making photography very difficult.

Seven Mile Reef

This reef is some 11 km (7 miles) north of Jesser Point, just beyond the Parks Board beacon and about 3 km from the shore. It is a small reef where the average depth is 25 m. Being fairly difficult to find it is enjoyed by those few who know its location. Sharks and the larger game fish are often sighted here.

Nine Mile Reef

In contrast Nine Mile is easy to find. It is located 15 km (9 miles) north of Jesser Point and starts just beyond the first point outside the Sodwana reserve. It can be seen from a boat as the swells often break over the reef. Boat divers should be wary of the breaking waves and anchor in the deeper water on the seaward side of the reef. Nine Mile is regarded by many as the most beautiful and spectacular reef off Sodwana: it rises from a depth of 20 m to less than 1 m at its peak. This sloping rock wall is filled with caves, some of them huge, and is covered with coral. It is a living mass of fish and the larger game fish and sharks can be seen cruising along the outer side of the wall. Closer to the shore there are a number of small rocky reefs, very interesting to explore. On a calm day scuba divers are able to swim out to the reef from the shore, a swim of approximately 1 km.

Mabibi

About 25 km north of Jesser Point is a bay called Mabibi, which is at the northern limit of permitted beach travel. For snorkellers the inshore rocky area provides magnificent deep pools full of coral fish. At low tide these pools are protected from the sea by a natural rocky wall. Directly off shore there are several rocky reefs which run parallel to the coast, shallow at first and later falling to a depth of 30 m. The deep area provides excellent diving similar to that of Seven Mile. A little further north is a large coral reef inhabited by many potato bass and also attracting a fair share of sharks. Mabibi provides some spectacular diving and no visit to Sodwana is complete without a visit here.

About 2 km south of Mabibi is a small but beautiful rocky reef hosting many of the larger reef fish such as the baardman. Further south and covering several kilometres is an area known as the kelp beds. They are flat limestone beds about 100 m wide and covered in seaweed. Many species of fish not normally seen on the deeper coral are found here and on a calm day it is possible to drift dive over the beds and take unusual photographs.

ISLAND ROCK/KOSI BAY

Some 10 km north of Mabibi is Island Rock and still further north, Kosi Bay. Both provide excellent diving, Kosi in particular, but boating and other restrictions make these places inaccessible to most divers.

LEVERN POINT/LEDSMAN SHOAL

This is easily the best diving site off the South African coast and is situated about 15 km north of Cape Vidal. This area has recently been proclaimed a marine sanctuary and may now only be dived for scientific and research purposes, and then only with a permit.

ALIWAL SHOALS

Aliwal Shoals, off the Natal coast between Umkomaas and Scottburgh, is another area highly rated by divers. The shoal is mainly rock but has many isolated coral outcrops, making it one of the southernmost coral areas in the world. It is fairly difficult to reach as it is 7 km from the shore and launching boats off this area of the coast is not easy. The reef rises from 50 m on the outer edge to 2 m at its pinnacle and runs parallel to the shore for 4 km or 5 km. On a good day the visibility can be up to 50 m and tremendous diving can be had. This is not for beginners and dives here must only be attempted with locals who know the area well, as the currents can be treacherous. Although Aliwal offers excellent diving, the conditions are seldom good and many a diving trip arranged for this area has to be aborted.

North of Aliwal and closer to shore is the wreck of the *Produce* sitting upright on the bottom in about 30 m of water. This is a superb diving site inhabited by several huge brindlebass, up to 400 kg each and in winter by large shoals of salmon. The wreck is difficult to locate and expert navigation is required.

HABITS AND HABITATS

The authors have observed some interesting general behaviour patterns of fish which can be shared with readers to make their discovery and identification of the different species easier.

THE CORAL REEF INHABITANTS

This is generally the group of fish on which divers concentrate. Careful scientific studies have shown that within such a coral reef community, many fish exhibit fierce territorial behaviour, others are symbiotic and nearly all can co-exist harmoniously with their fellow inhabitants. The coral reef is probably the most complicated ecosystem in the world and it is often difficult to distinguish its permanent inhabitants from those just passing by. More than half the fish appearing in this book inhabit coral reefs.

THE CAVE DWELLERS

The non-coral reefs off the South African coast are mostly composed of limestone which, because of the abrasive wave action, contains wonderful cave formations. These provide many species with shelter. Most of the Sodwana coral reefs are built on limestone and many caves can be found at Nine Mile and Mabibi. Rockcod, river snapper (rock salmon), kob and even kingfish can be found in these caves, together with many of the smaller coral reef species and the nocturnal feeders. Exploring these caves requires a certain amount of care and underwater torches are recommended.

THE WATER COLUMN INHABITANTS

An interesting phenomenon, well known to spearfishermen, is the behavioural patterns of some reef fish, which spend their time when certain conditions prevail in the water column above or near a reef. Old women, spadefish, Englishmen, steenbras, Mozambique knifejaw (cuckoo bass) and many others congregate in the column and feed on passing plankton. Most reefs on the east coast run parallel to the shore and when the current is running north to south, the aggregations can be found on the northern end of the reef, and vice versa. This accumulation of fish, usually over sand, is normally focused near a cave area which provides shelter against threats.

THE OPEN SEA INHABITANTS

Pelagic game fish can be found almost anywhere and they too exhibi distinct behavioural patterns. Certain species such as garrick, yellow tail and snoek are often found close to the shore just behind the last lin of breakers or in the deep channel that runs close to the beach. The kin mackerel or cuda, as it is known locally, may be seen swimming clos to the surface when the current is flowing from the north; on a chang it may be found along the sand at a depth of 25 m to 30 m.

UNDERWATER PHOTOGRAPHY

Most of the photographs in this book were taken off the Natal coast and particularly on the Sodwana Bay reefs. Underwater photography is not easy even if the conditions are perfect. Those readers who have travelled will know about the flat calm seas of romantic holiday spots like the Red Sea, Mauritius, Seychelles and the Maldives. Sodwana is not like them, which makes the challenge of obtaining good pictures that much greater.

The seas off the northern Natal coast are seldom flat. There is usually a swell running and the Mozambique current can flow at a rate of up to 4 knots. The swell leads to fairly severe surges underwater which can at times carry a diver 10 m in a direction in which he may or may not want to go. The surge can also churn up the ocean bed, thus reducing visibility.

Taking these pictures was a lot of fun, but not without incident and pain. One method of trying to capture a fish on film is to try to drift just above the fish, following it through the viewfinder until it is framed correctly, then pressing the shutter. While this makes sense one should remember that everything through the viewfinder is distorted and things appear further away than they really are. Many times one will cruise in over a fish only to crash into a coral head and come away cut and bleeding — needless to say, a painful experience. The surges will often throw the diver onto the rocks and great care must be taken to protect the equipment.

Another, often better, method is to wedge oneself into the rocks and wait for the fish to pass. As many of the fish are usually found in the back of caves and crevasses, some contortions may be required in order to get the right camera angle and lighting.

The equipment used for photographs in this book was all Nikonos: the cameras were Nikonos II, IVA and V; the flashes were Nikonos SB101 Speedlights, probably the best underwater 35 mm camera equipment available for these conditions. The equipment is very rugged, which is essential, as it takes a hammering both underwater and in transportation on the boat. Here care must be taken to ensure the equipment is well secured away from things like weight belts and diving tanks.

Lighting poses a serious problem for the underwater photographer. Colours fade as the depth of water increases, with reds and yellows disappearing first. At about 30 m below the surface, only blues are left. In addition the amount of natural light that penetrates below the surface is determined by the clarity of the water and the angle of the sun. For these reasons it is necessary to use underwater lighting, usually a flash gun. When taking a photograph against coral or in a cave, there is a tendency to overexposure as the light from the flash bounces back off the coral. In this instance the power of the flash has to be reduced: a quarter power is recommended for such shots. This setting is also recommended for pictures of silver or light-coloured fish. For a fish swimming in the mid-water more power should be used, but care must be taken as the light from the flash will bounce off the plankton and other suspended matter in the water and spots will appear in the picture. To prevent this the flash should not be mounted on the camera but held at arm's length to the side. This poses another difficulty in ensuring that the light is pointing at the subject, but the advantage is that the plankton and other matter will be less evident.

As objects appear larger underwater than they really are, focusing requires experience as distances are difficult to estimate. Using 200 or 400 ASA film allows a smaller aperture to be used and hence a bigger depth of field to be achieved.

Most of the pictures in this book were taken with a standard 35 mm lens, except for a few taken with a close-up kit which is ideal for smaller fish but has an incredibly shallow depth of field.

Alas, most fish don't cooperate with the photographer and will continually dart around, making framing a difficult task. However, there is a lot of satisfaction gained in getting the right picture provided one realises that there will be many failures. Persevere and the rewards will be forthcoming.

WHALE SHARK
Walvishaai
Rhincodon typus (8.1)

DESCRIPTION (size: up to 15 m)
The whale shark is the largest of all living fishes and therefore almost unnecessary to describe. It is dark blue-grey or brown with white spots and vertical stripes. The lower part of the body is a light shade of grey with no distinguishing markings.

HABITAT
Often found cruising slowly just below the surface in clean water with its dorsal fin and offset tail just protruding above the surface.

FEEDING HABITS
Like its bigger "brother" the whale, it is a filter feeder, eating large quantities of plankton and small fish.

GENERAL
The sighting of this fish has to be one of the greatest thrills to divers. It is not normally aggressive and will allow one to hang onto its huge dorsal fin and be towed along. At this stage care must be taken as its size belies its speed and a mask can easily be torn off if one turns one's head sideways. The only potential danger lies in its huge bulk and the power of the tail; the latter should be avoided.

SPOTTED RAGGED-TOOTH

Spikkel-skeurtandhaai

Eugomphodus taurus (19.1)

DESCRIPTION (size: up to 3 m)

The "raggie", as it is commonly and affectionately known, looks more ungainly than most sharks, appearing short and squat with a hump-back and little "piggy" eyes. However, it can move surprisingly quickly if disturbed. It is brown or sometimes grey, lighter under-neath. The tip of the tail often looks as if it has been broken. It gets its name from and can usually be recognised by an ugly set of teeth that are more visible than in most other sharks.

HABITAT

The ragged-tooth is usually seen in shallower water than other sharks, in gullies or in caves, particularly off Sodwana point, where it can often be seen cruising lazily over the reef in search of food in the late afternoon or early morning.

FEEDING HABITS

The ragged-tooth feeds on slow-swimming or any other fish, such as small sharks and rays.

GENERAL

Although not regarded as aggressive it is likely to attack skin divers

carrying speared fish. Contrary to popular belief the ragged-tooth is able, through gill movements, to ensure constant flow of water over the gills and thus breathe while remaining motionless. Its habit of lying motionless in a gully often causes great consternation to divers who come across one unexpectedly, although there have been no reports of an attack in these circumstances. As the first photograph shows the ragged-tooth blends well with a sandy or sandstone bottom. Mating occurs in the winter months off the Natal coast and usually two pups are born in the Cape 9–12 months later. The second photograph shows the ragged-tooth shape silhouetted.

SPOTTED EAGLERAY

Spikkel-arendrog

Aetobatus narinari (28.1)

DESCRIPTION (size: width to 2 m)

This ray is easily identified by its almost diamond-shaped body, dark blue or black above with regularly spaced white spots. The underside is white. It has a fleshy head with a protruding snout and a very long tail.

HABITAT

As with all rays it is often seen gliding gracefully in the mid-water above the reefs or sea bed.

FEEDING HABITS

Main diet consists of bivalves, shrimps, crabs, oysters and mussels.

GENERAL

The spotted eagleray is not regarded as aggressive to divers and can easily be approached underwater. It is particularly exciting to have one of these graceful fish swim overhead. Eaglerays have a stinging spine at the base of the tail. The photograph also shows several prodigal sons, which are described on p. 102.

HONEYCOMB STINGRAY (LEOPARD STINGRAY)

Heuningkoek-pylstert

Himantura uarnak (30.10)

DESCRIPTION (size: up to 2 m)
The upper side is brown or black with a honeycomb pattern outlined in white; the underside is white. It has a long whip-like tail which is usually two to three times the length of its body. Its body is wider than it is long. Both eyes are on the upper side of the body just in front of the two breathing holes, called spiracles.

HABITAT
Like many of its namesakes the honeycomb stingray usually lies half buried in the sand in or near a reef area. It can also be seen gliding gracefully over a reef or sand.

FEEDING HABITS
As a bottom swimmer it feeds on small crabs, prawns and other crustaceans.

GENERAL
As the honeycomb stingray often lies half buried in the sand it can be quite dangerous to divers who settle on what looks like a clear patch of sand only to find that the whole thing erupts and swims away — an unnerving experience for the unwary. In addition the stingray can

inflict painful wounds with its sharp spines, which are poisonous. Any wounds caused by a stingray should be treated by immersion in very hot water to reduce the effect of the protein toxin.

ROUND RIBBONTAILRAY

Ronde lintstertrog

Taeniura melanospilos (30.14)

DESCRIPTION (size: width up to 2 m)

The round ribbontailray, also known as the fantail, grows to a substantial size, a specimen of over 150 kg having been caught off the Natal coast. It is circular in shape; mostly blue-grey or black on top and white underneath. The fleshy tail is usually no longer than the body and lacks the stinging capability of the stingray. The tail distinguishes this species from all the other species of ray and thus, if seen in the open, makes the round ribbontailray easy to identify.

HABITAT

This ray often buries itself in the sand, usually in a cave or under a ledge. It can be seen anywhere from the surf zone to depths of 500 m.

FEEDING HABITS

Because of its large wings it glides effortlessly over the reef or sand in search of prey such as crabs, prawns or bivalves.

GENERAL

Although not aggressive to divers it can be dangerous if inadvertently sat on: in its inevitable sudden movement it could severely bump and bruise the diver. They are easy to approach underwater.

HONEYCOMB MORAY
Heuningkoek-bontpaling
Gymnothorax favagineus (41.11)

DESCRIPTION (size: up to 2,5 m)
This eel is easy to identify: it is very large just behind the head and has a distinctive honeycomb pattern of yellow or white lines on a dark brown body, which gives it its name. It has powerful jaws and looks quite ferocious.

HABITAT
Normally seen in caves with only the head and thick neck protruding. It can however be seen swimming freely around Two Mile Reef at Sodwana.

FEEDING HABITS
It feeds on octopus and unsuspecting fish that venture too close to its cave.

GENERAL
Moray eels have a symbiotic relationship with crayfish, often sharing their cave with them. Octopus prey on the crayfish and provide a ready food source, a favourite for the moray. Moray eels are normally not aggressive to divers and can be hand-fed and stroked. However, they are likely to bite a hand suddenly thrust into their cave to forage

for crayfish. The first photograph shows the eel preening itself while being cleaned by two cleaner wrasse. At this stage the eel swells behind the head and gill areas and becomes quite coy.

The second photograph shows only the head of a honeycomb moray sticking out of its hole in a coral reef. Although its mouth is open the normally sharp teeth are depressed into the jaw and are not visible. Moray eels are frequently caught by fishermen off the rocks on the Natal coast and when pulled out of the water are very difficult to remove from the hook as they tie themselves in knots.

PINEAPPLE FISH
Pynappelvis
Monocentris japonicus (128.1)

DESCRIPTION (size: up to 17 cm)
As the name suggests, this fish bears a remarkable resemblance to a pineapple: the yellow body has black edges to the scales. The tail is translucent.

HABITAT
Usually found swimming in clear deep water just above the sea or reef bottom. As with many of the deep water swimmers this fish has light-generating organs, which are thought to be used to attract prey.

FEEDING HABITS
Feeds on small marine animals.

GENERAL
This interesting fish is rarely seen: it spends most daylight hours in dark caves, usually only emerging at night. Its scales are proportionately much larger than on other fish and form a formidable armour. Pineapple fish have an ancestry longer than the average fish and members of the family are known to have existed millions of years ago.

BLOTCHEYE SOLDIER
Vlekoog-soldaat
Myripristis murdjan (132.26)

DESCRIPTION (size: up to 27 cm)
The background colour of this fish is red with blackish edges to the gill covers. Above each eye is a dark blotch, hence the name. The fins are a darker red, edged in white.

HABITAT
As the picture shows it is often seen in small shoals in and around the reef. A primarily nocturnal fish, it is often found in the darker areas of the reef.

FEEDING HABITS
Feeds on crab larvae, shrimps and other small fish.

GENERAL
Very common at Sodwana Bay and easy to photograph. Unless frightened, blotcheye soldiers do not swim away from an underwater photographer.

DEEPWATER SOLDIER (HORNED SQUIRRELFISH)
Diepwater-soldaat

Ostichthys kaianus (Adioryx cornutus in Australia) (132.33)

DESCRIPTION (size: up to 20 cm)
It has a similar shape to the blotcheye. The body colour is pinky-red in front and fading to white towards the rear; there is a white line in a semi-circle behind the eye and another in front of the gill plate. The fins are opaque outlined in red. A characteristic of this species is the large preopercular spine.

HABITAT
It is not common and, being nocturnal, is seldom seen out in the open.

FEEDING HABITS
Carnivorous.

GENERAL
When seen it will probably be darting from one hole or cave to another, making it difficult to photograph.

TRUMPETFISH

Trompetvis

Aulostomus chinensis (143.1)

DESCRIPTION (size: up to 50 cm)

Although this fish is unmistakable, and the only one of its kind, it does have three distinct colour phases: bright yellow, grey with white markings and red with white and black markings. The pictures show the yellow and the grey/white varieties.

HABITAT

Can be seen swimming at different attitudes, horizontal or head down, in the mid-water. The head-down approach is used when concealing itself in the soft coral branches.

FEEDING HABITS

It feeds on other small fish and because of its long thin body shape tends to sneak up on its prey undetected.

GENERAL

It is common on coral reefs all around the world and the various colour phases determine the fish with which it hunts. For example, in its yellow phase it hunts with fish of a similar colour such as blue-banded snappers.

Like shrimpfish it often hovers in a head-down position, which

makes it easy to photograph when it is approached slowly; the only difficulty is getting the whole fish into the frame. It uses this pose, which gives it the appearance of seaweed, as one of its methods of attacking prey.

SMOOTH FLUTEMOUTH
Gladde fluitbek
Fistularia commersonii (144.1)

DESCRIPTION (size: up to 150 cm)
Although the overall body is elongated as in trumpetfish, the flute-mouth is quite different. Silvery with a green sheen on the upper half of the body, it has transparent dorsal, caudal and anal fins. The dorsal and anal fins are well to the rear of the body. The long tubular nose is very effective in sucking in its prey; the prominent black eyes are at the base of the nose.

HABITAT
The flutemouth is seen singly or in small groups cruising just below the surface or in mid-water above the coral reefs.

FEEDING HABITS
It feeds on small fish.

GENERAL
This fish is capable of swimming very fast and this, together with its length to depth ratio, makes it difficult to photograph.

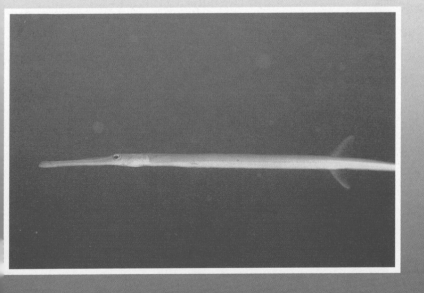

SHRIMPFISH (RAZOR FISH)

Garnaalvis

Aeoliscus punctulatus (148.1)

DESCRIPTION (size: up to 15 cm)
The body is grey overall with numerous black dots which give the impression of a dark band running lengthwise. The shrimpfish can appear translucent, an important aspect of its camouflage.

HABITAT
It is found swimming head down among sea grass and on sandy bottoms. A shoal of these can be mistaken for seaweed, as the photograph shows.

FEEDING HABITS
It feeds on very small crustaceans and larvae from the seabed.

GENERAL
These fish are highly manoeuvrable, able to propel themselves upwards, downwards and sideways. It is fascinating to encounter a group of these and, as seen in the photograph, they are not perturbed by the proximity of divers. However, if frightened they will turn horizontal and make off at high speed.

DEVIL FIREFISH
Duiwel-vuurvis
Pterois miles (149.8)

DESCRIPTION (size: up to 30 cm)
This is an unmistakable fish with long extended dorsal and pectoral fins. The overall colour varies from reddish to brown with vertical white lines on the body. There are several different species of firefish, difficult to distinguish from one another. The feature usually used to distinguish them is the colour and shape of the pectoral fins, which differ from species to species. In scientific terms the devil firefish is also called *Pterois volitans*.

HABITAT
This slow-moving fish is encountered in the protected areas of the reef, often in caves, and can be seen swimming upside down with sea goldies, as the photograph shows. Devil firefish are usually found in pairs and are seldom seen in the open during the day.

FEEDING HABITS
It normally feeds on slow-swimming creatures such as small crabs and shrimps which it gulps down. Because of its bewildering array of fins it is often mistaken by its prey for a harmless piece of floating seaweed.

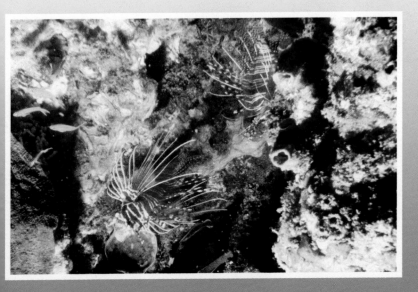

GENERAL

The firefish is common the world over and very easy to approach and photograph. It must be noted that the fins are extremely poisonous: wounds inflicted, while not fatal, can be very painful. Although usually very slow swimming, the firefish can move very quickly when attacking which it does with a backwards jumping motion bringing its very sharp dorsal fins into play.

The second photograph shows a pair of firefish drifting over the sand at the base of Nine Mile Reef. The devil firefish is highly prized by marine aquarists, since it is both easy to capture and easy to keep in captivity.

RAGGY SCORPIONFISH

Lappies-skerpioenvis

Scorpaenopsis venosa (149.36)

DESCRIPTION (size: up to 18 cm)
Sometimes confused with the stonefish (see following page) and part of the same family, the raggy scorpionfish does not, however, have the upturned mouth of the stonefish. The raggy is a mottled orange to rustic brown colour, with some green. It has distinctive protruding eyes.

HABITAT
Normally found motionless on the reef surface, often in the broken coral rubble.

FEEDING HABITS
Eats almost anything from small fish to crustaceans.

GENERAL
Like the stonefish it needs to be prodded in order to make it move. Because it is sluggish and normally motionless it is easy to photograph. It is very well camouflaged and the unwary diver runs the risk of inadvertently touching it. Fortunately the only harm will be a nasty dorsal spine puncture.

STONEFISH

Steenvis

Synanceia verrucosa (149.4

DESCRIPTION (size: up to 35 cm)
As the name suggests, this fish often looks like a stone: it adopts the colours of its surroundings. The huge pectoral fins are brilliantly coloured, mainly orange. These colours are not normally seen in the stationary fish. Because it lies still in one place for prolonged periods, it attracts barnacles which cover the head and back, adding to its stone-like appearance. Its mouth faces upwards in a half-moon shape and its eyes protrude from the head.

HABITAT
This solitary fish is found on the coral reef and is often overlooked as it really does look like a rock. It only swims if prodded — this to be done with extreme care, if at all.

FEEDING HABITS
Feeds on small fish which mistake its open mouth for the sanctuary of a rock cave, and pay the penalty.

GENERAL
A very poor swimmer because of its minute caudal fin, it appears almost to waddle when disturbed. This is the most venomous fish in

the ocean: its tough dorsal spines provide the most effective natural injection system of any marine animal. Wounds inflicted by it are extremely painful and potentially fatal. On the central African coast the locals treat such wounds by binding paw-paws over the affected areas. Paw-paws contain certain acids that break down the spines and protein poisons.

The second photograph shows the stonefish from the side and illustrates just how difficult it is to distinguish it from a rock.

SEA GOLDIE (ORANGE FAIRY BASSLET)
See-goudvissie
Anthias squamipinnis (166.9)

DESCRIPTION (size: up to 10 cm)

The fairy basslets are known as the jewels of the sea and the orange variety is common in all the tropical oceans of the world. The females are orange with a blue stripe below the eye; the males are darker have more reddish bodies and more pronounced fins, especially the dorsal filament. Both sexes can be distinguished in the photograph The second picture shows only a male sea goldie swimming upside-down in a cave.

HABITAT

They are very common and can be seen in large shoals in caves around coral bombies, drop-offs and ledges. As the picture shows they are frequently seen swimming upside down.

FEEDING HABITS

They feed on plankton and larval fish.

GENERAL

These fish are all born as females and change sex as and when males are required for spawning purposes. In any large shoal the majority will be female. The males are territorial and appear to keep up to 40

females in their harem. They spend much of their time and energy
chasing other males away. As sea goldies are easy to capture and
easy to keep in captivity they are prized by marine aquarists. They
make excellent photographic subjects as they are very tolerant of
divers. Because of their small size a close-up lens will produce a good
result.

CORAL ROCKCOD
Koraal-klipkabeljou
Cephalopholis miniata (166.26)

DESCRIPTION (size: up to 40 cm)
Sometimes mistaken for one of the coral trout, the coral rockcod can
be distinguished by its larger blue spots, its blue-edged fins, deeper
red colour and the rounded margin on the tail. It has orange pectoral
fins.

HABITAT
Individuals are normally seen in caves and coral labyrinths, down to
about 40 m, but may also be seen in the open.

FEEDING HABITS
It preys on small crabs and shrimps.

GENERAL
This fish is fairly common but not always easy to approach. It makes
excellent eating. Like all rockcod it has a hinged jaw allowing it to
swallow larger prey. It has very sharp gill rakers and should only be
handled with gloves.

CATFACE ROCKCOD

Katgesig-klipkabeljou

Epinephelus andersoni (166.34)

DESCRIPTION (size: up to 80 cm)
The basic body colour is brown entirely covered (with the exception of the head) with dark spots. The face has two or three oblique stripes which look like whiskers, hence the name. It has a very rounded caudal fin.

HABITAT
Found both in the shallows and on rocky reefs where it may be seen motionless waiting for prey.

FEEDING HABITS
Feeds on various small fish, crayfish and crabs.

GENERAL
It is common all along the Natal coast. A highly manoeuvrable fish, it proves difficult for spearfishermen to shoot, as it tends to lie on the bottom near its cave in a head-on position and the slightest movement causes it to dart away. Makes excellent eating.

BROWNSPOTTED ROCKCOD
Bruinspikkel-klipkabeljou
Epinephelus chlorostigma (166.38)

DESCRIPTION (size: up to 75 cm)
The light brown body is patterned with hexagonal brown blotches similar to those of the honeycomb moray. The underside of the brown-spotted rockcod tends to be paler. Its tail has a straight edge.

HABITAT
Solitary, it generally frequents the deeper coral reefs.

FEEDING HABITS
Carnivorous, feeding on small fish and crabs.

GENERAL
As with many of the rockcod, sex reversal occurs at a length of 37 cm; all individuals smaller than this are female. The brownspotted rock-cod makes very good eating. Elsewhere it is known as the birdwire rockcod and should not be confused with the greasy rockcod *(E.tau-vina)*, which is also known as the brownspotted rockcod.

REDBARRED ROCKCOD

Rooibalk-klipkabeljou

Epinephelus fasciatus (166.39)

DESCRIPTION (size: up to 35 cm)
This is one of the smaller varieties of rockcod. Its overall colour is reddish orange, the fins being more yellow. The flanks have four dark red bands running vertically.

HABITAT
Frequents rocky and coral reefs and can be seen lying motionless waiting for prey. It is shown here with a school of sea goldies.

FEEDING HABITS
Generally feeds on small fish, crabs and marine worms.

GENERAL
The redbarred rockcod can be found both on shallow and deep reefs, up to 160 m. It often lies in wait for prey on elevated platforms on the reef, ready to launch itself on some unsuspecting passer-by.

YELLOWTAIL ROCKCOD
Geelstert-klipkabeljou
Epinephelus flavocaeruleus (166.4

DESCRIPTION (size: up to 90 cm)
Very easily identified by the yellow fins and yellow upper lip. The
rest of the body is a dark grey/black and can be mottled with ligh
spots. As the fish grows older the yellow tends to fade and disappear

HABITAT
Unlike other rockcod this fish tends to hover in the mid-water above
the coral heads. Adults are solitary and frequent the deeper waters
while juveniles prefer the shallower areas.

FEEDING HABITS
Its diet consists mainly of other small reef fish, crayfish and crabs.

GENERAL
Although an excellent eating fish it is generally found too deep fo
spearfishermen, up to 150 m beneath the surface. Sex reversal occur
at a body length of 35 cm.

YELLOWBELLY ROCKCOD

Geelpens-klipkabeljou

Epinephelus guaza (166.43)

DESCRIPTION (size: up to 150 cm)
This large member of the rockcod family can be recognised by its distinctive "fat" shape. It is deep brown overall with irregular white blotches on its back; the belly is yellow and the fins are edged in yellow or orange. It has very sharp gill rakers and dorsal spines. Considerable colour variation can occur, from very light to very dark.

HABITAT
Solitary, it tends to live in caves in coral or rocky reefs and is often seen lying on the bottom near its cave.

FEEDING HABITS
It feeds on crayfish and other bottom-dwelling crustaceans.

GENERAL
This fish is found throughout the oceans of the world and was prolific in the Mediterranean prior to being fished out. Large numbers are caught by ski-boat and commercial fishermen off our coast. The photograph shows a yellowbelly struggling to free itself from a fisherman's line attached to the foot rope of a shark net. After taking its picture in this predicament, we were able to set it free. The yellow-

belly rockcod is good to eat; its firm white flesh tastes similar to that
of crayfish.

In the second photograph it is being cleaned by a cleaner wrasse,
hence the unusual attitude of the pectoral fin. As with the catface
rockcod, small yellow-bellies can be found in very shallow water in
rock pools as well as in bays and estuaries.

POTATO BASS

Aartappel-baars

Epinephelus tukula (166.66)

DESCRIPTION (size: up to 2 m)
The body is light brown/white with large dark spots. Large specimens can be almost totally dark brown or can appear almost white in certain conditions. Because of its size it can be mistaken for the brindlebass *(E.lanceolatus)* or the greasy rockcod *(E.tauvina)*, although both of these are bigger than the potato bass.

HABITAT
A very territorial fish, it can be seen swimming above coral and rocky reefs or darting into a cave when approached.

FEEDING HABITS
Eats reef fish and crustaceans. Like all members of the rockcod family, it sucks in its prey by forcibly expelling water through its large gill openings.

GENERAL
This fish is a divers' favourite. It is sometimes extremely inquisitive, to the point of becoming a nuisance. At Two Mile Reef at Sodwana one could meet "Archie": this resident potato bass was a friendly show-off and could be cuddled and stroked by divers. However,

being so friendly cost him his life at the hands of an unscrupulous spearfisherman. Others have now taken his place. Like its larger cousin the giant grouper or brindlebass the potato bass has been protected for many years, first by an unwritten pact between the divers themselves and more recently by legislation.

Being extremely territorial the potato bass can become quite aggressive to unwelcome visitors. Jacques Cousteau, the world-famous underwater explorer, conducted an experiment in an attempt to understand this behaviour. He repeatedly placed on the sea-bed a large mirror, within the bounds of the territory of a potato bass. Every time the potato bass would rush at the mirror and repeatedly smash into it until the mirror shattered.

The second photograph shows the relative size of a potato bass when compared with a young diver.

YELLOW-EDGE LYRETAIL (SWALLOWTAIL ROCKCOD)
Geelrand-maanstert
Variola louti (166.75)

DESCRIPTION (size: up to 80 cm)
The overall colour is bright red and the body is covered with blue or purple blotches. The fins are blue spotted with bright yellow margins. When the fish is being cleaned the spots tend to disappear and the colour can be almost crimson. The tail is easily recognised by its deep V shape and long trailing filaments.

HABITAT
Caves and deep gullies on the reefs.

FEEDING HABITS
It prefers small fish such as soldiers and cardinals but will also eat small crustaceans.

GENERAL
This beautiful fish, common off the Natal coast, is not easy to photograph. Wary of divers, the yellow-edge lyretail, unless found at a cleaner wrasse station, usually presents the photographer with a rear view of its long tailfins as it dives under a ledge or into a cave.

SIXSTRIPE SOAPFISH
Sesstreep-seepvis
Grammistes sexlineatus (167.3)

DESCRIPTION (size: up to 25 cm)
The body is dark brown with yellow stripes running along the length
of the body. In the larger adults the stripes tend to break up.

HABITAT
It tends to be found beneath coral ledges and in caves.

FEEDING HABITS
Carnivorous, feeding on crustaceans and small fish.

GENERAL
It is a popular aquarium fish but care must be taken when introducing
it to other small fish. When frightened or threatened in any way it gives
off a toxin.

DUTOITI

Dutoiti

Pseudochromis dutoiti (169.4)

DESCRIPTION (size: up to 9 cm)
This small yet pretty fish is a tan colour that tends to redden towards the tail. All fins are edged in blue with darker inserts. A V-shaped blue line runs from the point of the head to join the dorsal rays.

HABITAT
It is common, although rather timid, and seen in the shallower coral and rocky reef areas. Often seen in tidal pools.

FEEDING HABITS
Feeds on very small crustaceans and plankton.

GENERAL
This fish is regarded as one of the jewels among the smaller coral reef fishes. It is highly prized by marine aquarists. The dutoiti is not a fast mover and can easily be caught in a small net.

GLASS BIGEYE
Glas-grootoog
Priacanthus cruentatus (174.2)

DESCRIPTION (size: up to 30 cm)
Colour silvery with a pinkish hue and numerous red blotches; the fins are covered in red spots. It has a very large eye as it is primarily nocturnal. The mouth is distinctively upturned.

HABITAT
As the photograph shows it is usually found lying motionless under plate coral or in a cave during the day.

FEEDING HABITS
Carnivorous, eating free-swimming crustaceans and cephalopods.

GENERAL
Being nocturnal, it is rarely seen during the day. When foraging at night it may be seen away from the reef over sand or coral rubble.

CRESCENT-TAIL BIGEYE
Sekelstert-grootoog
Priacanthus hamrur (174.3)

DESCRIPTION (size: up to 45 cm)
Colour basically silver, with tinges of pink on the upper part of the body. The tail, anal and dorsal fins are opaque, with the caudal fin having a black margin. Like the previous species it has a distinctive large eye and upturned mouth.

HABITAT
It can be found in the coral reefs but not in the open.

FEEDING HABITS
Carnivorous, eating free-swimming crustaceans and cephalopods.

GENERAL
Being nocturnal, it is rarely seen during the day. It may emerge in the late afternoon, when this photograph was taken, but will stay close to the coral.

LEMONFISH

Lemmetjievis

Plectorhinchus flavomaculatus (179.3)

DESCRIPTION (size: up to 60 cm)
This fish is beautifully marked: the overall colour is grey with extensive yellow spots; these fuse at the face into a wavy line. The base of the pectoral fins is orange.

HABITAT
Common in our waters, this bottom dweller is usually seen near reefs and rocky outcrops.

FEEDING HABITS
Feeds on bottom-dwelling invertebrates.

GENERAL
This fish makes excellent eating and, being a sluggish swimmer, makes an easy target for spearfishermen. However, if not squarely struck the soft flesh will not hold a spear and hence it is possible to see lemonfish as well as other rubberlips with spear marks in the dorsal area. The lemonfish can be quite inquisitive and will approach divers. Those found off the Natal coast seldom have a mass of more than 2 kg, which is below the minimum limit for the spearfishing of marine fish.

WHITEBARRED RUBBERLIP
Witbalk-rubberlip
Plectorhinchus playfairi (179.7)

DESCRIPTION (size: up to 90 cm)
As seen from the picture this fish is unmistakable: the body is dark above, white below with three very distinct white vertical bars. A fourth bar runs down the head. Both the fat lips and the interior of the mouth are pink.

HABITAT
Usually a solitary swimmer, although several may be found in the same area around rocky and coral reefs.

FEEDING HABITS
Feeds on small fish and small invertebrates.

GENERAL
Although common this is a timid fish and not easily approached underwater. It makes excellent eating but care must be taken as the flesh spoils very quickly.

MINSTREL (GREY SWEETLIPS)
Minstreel
Plectorhinchus schotaf (179.8)

DESCRIPTION (size: up to 40 cm)
This fish is difficult to distinguish from its cousins the redlip rubberlip, the dusky rubberlip and even the sailfin rubberlip, known elsewhere as the painted sailfin. All three are nearly uniformly grey in
adult form, so the traditional scientific methods of counting dorsal
spines and gill rakers are usually the best means of positive identification. The minstrel, however, has a very dark pink (almost scarlet)
colour in the interior of its mouth and along the edges of the gill
covers.

HABITAT
Normally seen in shoals of 5 to 50 around coral or rocky reefs in the
company of other reef fish such as the old woman, Mozambique
knifejaw (cuckoo bass) and cod.

FEEDING HABITS
The primary diet consists of small invertebrates.

GENERAL
These communities of reef fish are a common phenomenon off the
South African coast, where it is often possible to swim even in reef

areas for considerable distances without seeing fish in numbers and then to come upon an area densely populated with these and other species.

Making almost no effort at first to avoid divers, the minstrel is an easy fish to spear but after several have been speared in the same area, the shoal becomes agitated and like a baardman shoal will try to avoid the spearfisherman. Like the baardman, the minstrel has very soft flesh and consequently a spear not properly placed will easily tear out. The flesh of all rubberlips spoils quickly, particularly if left in the hot sun.

The second photograph, taken without light on the deep part of Nine Mile Reef, shows a small group of minstrels of between 2 kg and 4 kg each.

RIVER SNAPPER (ROCK SALMON)

Rivier-snapper

Lutjanus argentimaculatus (181.5)

DESCRIPTION (size: up to 100 cm)

The river snapper or rock salmon, as it is known to divers, is often described in the literature as being coppery-red; however, the live fish is usually somewhere between a light maroon and an ever lighter grey. It has several large vicious-looking teeth and very sharp gill rakers similar to those of the rockcod family. Like many of the snappers it makes a distinctive clicking noise with its jaw, hence the name.

HABITAT

Usually found on most reefs along the Natal and Transkei coasts either singly or in small shoals. It enjoys the company of other reef fish such as rockcod, chub and rubberlips and prefers a reef area with large caves into which it disappears at speed when hunted. When in the cave it is almost impossible to see, blending with the rock or coral; however, the beating of its large tail can be heard as it moves around, never remaining still for a second.

FEEDING HABITS

It eats a variety of reef fish, crabs and crayfish.

GENERAL

Divers, particularly spearfishermen, know this magnificent fighting fish as one of the most difficult reef fish in the sea to spear. In Australia it is well known as the mangrove jack as it inhabits and breeds in the estuaries along the coast. When speared this fish dives for the nearest cave or coral reef and if allowed to get there, ties up the line and tears itself off the spear unless mortally wounded. It is a brave or foolhardy spearfisherman who tries to shoot a rock salmon in a cave as this almost inevitably results in the loss of the spear or even the gun.

Both photographs are of small snappers (less than 2 kg). It is very difficult to approach river snappers larger than this, as most spearfishermen know. The second photograph, taken without artificial light, shows the distinct white marks on the tips of the caudal and anal fins.

HUMPBACK SNAPPER (PADDLE-TAIL)

Boggel-snapper

Lutjanus gibbus (181.10)

DESCRIPTION (size: up to 40 cm)

In local literature this fish is known as the humpback snapper whereas elsewhere its common name is paddle-tail. Under the water this fish seems a light silver colour with brown to black fins trimmed in white, a yellow upper lip, a bright yellow patch at the base of the dorsal fin and some yellow on the gill covers. The second photograph shows a much redder version of the same species which is closer to the description given in *A Guide to the Common Sea Fishes of Southern Africa* by Rudy van der Elst. Out of water it takes on an overall reddish colour with its fins edged in white. The fish gets its alternative common name from a broad and paddle-like tail, recurving at the tips.

HABITAT

Common in the coral reef areas in small shoals. It can be seen in the beautiful reefs close inshore just south of Mabibi.

FEEDING HABITS

Like other members of the snapper family it feeds during the night on small crustaceans.

GENERAL

Unlike the bluebanded snapper, the paddle-tail is often quite difficult to get close to, even when there are shoals about. It darts about
and is often very skittish, even camera shy. Occasionally, as the
photographs show, it stops and poses with surprisingly good
results. The paddle-tail should not be eaten as it has in some cases,
particularly in tropical waters, been held responsible for cases of
ciguatera poisoning.

BLUEBANDED SNAPPER
Blouband-snapper
Lutjanus kasmira (181.11)

DESCRIPTION (size: up to 33 cm)
The bluebanded snapper is the most colourful of the common Indian Ocean snapper family, being easily distinguished by its bright yellow colour and four vivid blue longitudinal stripes. Some fish have a dark blotch just below the dorsal fin rays.

HABITAT
Found in large shoals on most coral or rocky reefs at depths of 10-50 m. During the day the shoals are often seen hanging almost motionless over a rocky outcrop whereas in the late afternoon or early morning they are seen in smaller groups, feeding.

FEEDING HABITS
Feeds on small shrimps, crabs and other small fish.

GENERAL
This snapper is seldom disturbed by divers and when moving the shoal will divide and pass on both sides of the intruder. The shoals of blue-banded snapper often have one or more of the similar species, the one-spot or Russell's snapper, swimming with them. The photograph shows them swimming with a threadfin butterflyfish and a pencilled

surgeon. Snappers are voracious feeders and divers can easily hand feed them with fish or crayfish. A large shoal feeding in this way produces a kaleidoscope of colour. It is best to wear a glove when feeding fish like this as their sharp teeth can cause painful nips. Both photographs are of the same shoal.

BLUE-AND-GOLD FUSILIER

Blou-en-goue piesangvis

Caesio caerulaureus (182.1)

DESCRIPTION (size: up to 27 cm)
The entire fish has a sheen about it. It is pinky silver below and has a dark longitudinal band running through the upper caudal tail fin.

HABITAT
Normally found swimming in large shoals in the mid-water above the reef.

FEEDING HABITS
Carnivorous, feeding on zooplankton.

GENERAL
When these fish are encountered underwater the diver might suddenly find himself overwhelmed in a large shoal. Surprisingly, however, they never actually bump the diver. These fish are preyed upon in the early morning and late afternoon by the larger kingfish and other game fish, during which period they move swiftly and frequently break the water surface in their attempts to escape.

BEAUTIFUL FUSILIER
Pragtige piesangvis
Caesio teres (182.2)

DESCRIPTION (size: up to 30 cm)
The yellow covers the back and extends through to the base of the tail.
The nape and the top of the head are blue, the bottom half is silvery.
A blue band runs longitudinally between the yellow and silver por-
tions of the body.

HABITAT
Usually found in small shoals swimming in the mid-water above the
reef.

FEEDING HABITS
Carnivorous, feeding on zooplankton and small invertebrates.

GENERAL
This particularly beautiful fish is common in the Sodwana area. When
at cleaner stations it adopts a tail-standing attitude and turns a darker
blue.

ENGLISHMAN

Engelsman

Chrysoblephus anglicus (183.8)

DESCRIPTION (size: up to 100 cm)

The almost ruddy complexion and solemn looks of this fish gave rise to its common name. It is an overall silver/pinkish colour with six to eight darker red crossbars on the sides of the body. The dorsal and pectoral fins are distinctly pink and the tail a little darker. It has a very flat forehead, almost vertical, and a large pinkish eye.

HABITAT

The Englishman is seen in deeper water, either individually or in small groups, along with spadefish, etc. It is free swimming, ranging over large areas when feeding. When the current is flowing strongly on Aliwal Shoals or on the deeper reefs off the Natal coast and Sodwana these types of fish form a column on the upcurrent side of the reef where they face into the current and feed on the plankton as it passes. When there is little current the Englishman is found off the reef foraging in the sand for crustaceans, as seen in the second photograph.

FEEDING HABITS

It feeds on crabs, shrimps, squid and other small fish as well as plankton.

GENERAL

This well-known angling species is one of a family of tasty deepwater fish and is a firm favourite with ski-boat and commercial anglers off the Natal and Transkei coasts, often being boated in large numbers. The fish is quite difficult to get close to, drifting at a safe distance from a diver when in open water, but is curious about sand stirred up from the bottom.

WILDEPERD (ZEBRA)

Wildeperd

Diplodus cervinus hottentotus (183.16)

DESCRIPTION (size: up to 60 cm)

The wildeperd is silvery with five broad black vertical bars on the body. It often takes on a coppery-golden hue, which may be related to age or diet. It also has a black bar through each eye. Its pointed snout is useful for foraging; it is predominantly a vegetarian in its adult form.

HABITAT

Usually seen in fairly shallow water, being at home in the turbulent rocky surf zone as well as in the deeper waters of the rock and coral reefs.

FEEDING HABITS

In its adult form it feeds mainly on seaweed; juveniles are carnivorous.

GENERAL

The wildeperd is prolific on the east coast between Cape Town and Durban and contrary to what is shown in scientific works is frequently seen at Sodwana Bay and even as far north as Mozambique. It is easy to approach as it moves around the reef foraging on various plant forms. North of Nine Mile Reef at Sodwana Bay in the kelp beds

there are many specimens to be seen as this area makes excellent feeding for them. It is caught by surf anglers as well as ski-boat fishermen and occasionally a larger one is speared by a diver. The flesh is fairly palatable and is a staple food for the Indian community on the Natal coast, along with karranteen, blacktail and shad (elf). The wildeperd is also used as live bait by gamefishermen when angling for garrick, kingfish and cuda from the rocks on the east coast of southern Africa.

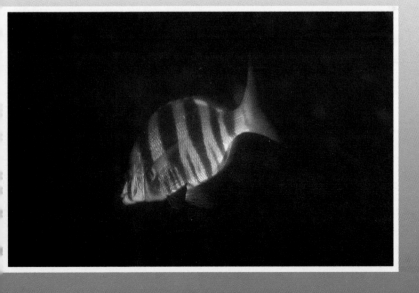

CAPE STUMPNOSE

Kaapse stompneus

Rhabdosargus holubi (183.36)

DESCRIPTION (size: up to 40 cm)
This deep-bodied fish has an overall silver sheen. A yellow band runs longitudinally along the mid-line of the body.

HABITAT
A very common inhabitant in both the shallow water and deep reefs.

FEEDING HABITS
It only feeds on the sandy bottom and will both graze and feed on small molluscs, crabs and shrimps.

GENERAL
As with many silver fish, the cape stumpnose is generally of little interest to divers. However, a large shoal, which is uncommon, can make a spectacular sight and if seen head on, an unusual photograph.

NATAL STUMPNOSE

Natalse stompneus

Rhabdosargus sarba (183.37)

DESCRIPTION (size: up to 80 cm)

This fish is similar to the Cape stumpnose but does not have the yellow mid-line band. It is silvery grey overall with a glint at the edge of each scale; collectively they show as grey longitudinal lines. The belly, pelvic, pectoral and anal fins are yellow although this fades with age.

HABITAT

Usually found swimming over the sand close to the shoreline although it will sometimes venture into the reef areas. It breeds in the estuaries along the Natal coast.

FEEDING HABITS

It is a bottom feeder; using its strong teeth it feeds on oysters, clams and other shellfish.

GENERAL

It is partial to sea lice and is frequently caught on this bait along the Durban beaches in the summer months. A strong swimmer, it fights well on light tackle. It is a prized table fish and one of the staples of the Indian community.

BLUE EMPEROR
Blou keiser
Lethrinus nebulosus (185.13)

DESCRIPTION (size: up to 75 cm)
The body tends to be a drab olive colour fading to a paler underside.
The pectoral fins are pinkish and the face has intricate patterns and markings.

HABITAT
Coral and rocky reefs, normally in the deeper water.

FEEDING HABITS
Diet consists of small crabs, worms and molluscs.

GENERAL
This fish is seldom seen by divers although common off the Natal coast, maybe because it tends to remain motionless over the reef and from above is not easily spotted. It is also known to divers and fishermen by the names scavenger and mata-hari as are several others of this genus. It is a prized table fish.

LONGFIN BATFISH
Langvin-vlermuisvis
Platax teira (192.3)

DESCRIPTION (size: up to 50 cm)
The overall rounded shape contributed to by the broad anal and dorsal fins makes this fish fairly easy to identify. Remarkable changes in shape occur between the juvenile and adult forms. Juveniles have long orange dorsal and anal fins; the pectoral fins in the adult are yellow. The body has vertical dark and light bands, one of which passes through the eye.

HABITAT
Always a mid-water swimmer, it is often seen in shoals in the water column with spadefish, cuckoo bass and Englishmen. A large shoal can usually be seen at Sodwana point.

FEEDING HABITS
Omnivorous, feeding on algae, salpas, sea jellies and plankton.

GENERAL
A very graceful swimmer and easily approached by divers, it makes an excellent photographic subject if found in clear water. It is not regarded as a good eating fish.

SPADEFISH
Graafvis
Tripterodon orbis (192.4)

DESCRIPTION (size: up to 50 cm)
This common reef fish is a silvery brown with dark vertical bands more prominent towards the front. It has a touch of yellow on the dorsal fin and tail.

HABITAT
A mid-water swimmer that inhabits the water column, frequently in small groups. Juveniles are commonly found over the sand just behind the breaking waves.

FEEDING HABITS
It feeds on mid-water invertebrates as well as nibbling encrusting organisms on the reef itself.

GENERAL
An inquisitive fish and easily approached underwater. Its large plate-like shape makes it an easy target for spearfishermen, but it is very bony and not particularly tasty. It is very manoeuvrable and has no difficulty moving in and out of the reef.

TWO-SADDLE GOATFISH

Tweesaal-bokvis

Parupeneus bifasciatus (196.4)

DESCRIPTION (size: up to 30 cm)
The fish is predominantly white with two dark vertical bars (saddles) tapering towards the bottom of the body.

HABITAT
Although usually solitary the two-saddle goatfish may be found resting in groups on the bottom in hollows in the reef. It may also be seen swimming away from the reef close to the sand.

FEEDING HABITS
In the early morning it forages in the sand pockets in the reef, searching for crustaceans and sea worms.

GENERAL
It is fairly common off Sodwana and easy to approach.

KOB (KABELJOU)

Kob

Argyrosomus hololepidotus (199.1)

DESCRIPTION (size: up to 2 m)
The body is silvery with a row of white spots running longitudinally along the lateral line. There is a pearly pink sheen on the head, flanks and dorsal surface.

HABITAT
Swims in shoals on the sandy edges of the reef and has been known to attain depths of 400 m. It is normally found off the Natal coast in the winter months when following the sardines up from the Cape.

FEEDING HABITS
It eats small fish and crustaceans.

GENERAL
The kob is one of the most common eating fish in South Africa and is caught all along our coast. It is very shy and seldom seen by divers although sometimes the sound made by the tails of a large shoal can be heard. Photographing or spearing the fish is extremely difficult. Large shoals of kob can be found on many deep reefs and wrecks and on rare occasions these fish will allow divers to mingle with them without rushing off as they do in shallow water. Large solitary

specimens are often found close to shore at rocky points such as the sandspit at Port Shepstone or Clansthall. Shoals of up to 1 000 fish have been seen by divers on wrecks such as the *Produce* near Aliwal Shoals.

In the winter huge catches of kob are made by ski-boat and commercial line fishermen off the deep reefs and wrecks along the Durban, Bluff and South Coast beaches. The authors have seen ski-boats returning to their bases so loaded that if the motors were stopped they would sink. As with other species there must be some concern that overfishing could deplete the apparently plentiful shoals of this important fish.

BAARDMAN (TASSELFISH)

Baardman

Umbrina canariensis (199.8)

DESCRIPTION (size: up to 55 cm)
A fairly deep-bodied fish, greyish brown in colour with a number o
silver stripes running along the body and angled slightly upwards. I
gets its name from a small protuberance or tassel under the chin, whic
could be construed as a beard.

HABITAT
This fish can be seen solitarily or in shoals, swimming above rock
reefs or in sandy gullies and caves. It is usually found inshore where i
feeds on the sand. Here the body colour becomes lighter, making it ver
difficult to see.

FEEDING HABITS
It feeds primarily on small bottom-dwelling invertebrates.

GENERAL
Easy to approach underwater. Some of the large shoals that inhabite
the inshore reefs north of Sodwana Bay were decimated prior to bein
protected. Like the rubberlips they are often seen with scars in th
dorsal area, caused by spears.

THREESPOT ANGELFISH
Driekol-engelvis
Apolemichthys trimaculatus (204.2)

DESCRIPTION (size: up to 25 cm)
Yellow with bright blue lips; the anal fin edged in black. Named for the three black spots: one on the forehead and one on either side of the body just behind the gills.

HABITAT
Regularly seen swimming in and around the coral reefs, usually in the shallower areas. Normally solitary although pairs or threes have been seen.

FEEDING HABITS
Eats algae.

GENERAL
This pretty fish is very shy and seems to object to being photographed, always twisting and turning to present an awkward view.

EMPEROR ANGELFISH
Keiser-engelvis
Pomacanthus imperator (204.9)

DESCRIPTION (size: up to 40 cm)
The adult form is spectacular, having 20-30 parallel yellow lines along
its length on a background of purple. The rear fins including the tail
are orange and the pectoral fins and surrounds are dark brown or
black. The mouth is white, the eye set in a black band edged with a
blue line. The anal fin is edged with blue. The juvenile is totally different: it is much more rounded, navy blue to almost black with con-
centric blue-white lines making it look like some weirdly coloured
dartboard. The *imperator* is arguably the most beautiful fish to be
seen in Natal and Zululand waters.

HABITAT
Usually found around coral and rocky reefs; normally solitary.

FEEDING HABITS
It feeds on sponges, algae and coral polyps.

GENERAL
This magnificent fish never fails to impress and can be quite inquisitive. At times it will pose beautifully for a photograph and at other
times it will prove most elusive. It is a popular aquarium fish, par-

icularly in its juvenile form: the adult requires too much space for
home aquariums.

Angelfish are found on coral reefs throughout the world and are,
almost without exception, the group of fish that divers and particu-
arly underwater photographers are most attracted to.

SEMICIRCLE ANGELFISH
Halfsirkel-engelvis
Pomacanthus semicirculatus (204.11)

DESCRIPTION (size: up to 50 cm)

The adult is very impressive, greenish overall and flecked with dark blue/black spots. All the fins are edged in bright blue as are the gills and the top of the eye. As seen from the second photograph the juvenile is quite different. Its body is navy blue to black with light blue/white stripes running vertically in curves down the body. It can easily be confused with the juvenile emperor angelfish which has the same colouring but whose curved stripes are almost circular. It is even more difficult to distinguish between the juvenile semicircle and the juvenile old woman. There may even be some confusion in *Smiths' Sea Fishes* in this regard.

HABITAT

It can be seen swimming along the surface and gullies of the reef. The juveniles are more likely to hide in the back of caves.

FEEDING HABITS

Feeds on sponges, small pieces of sessile plants and animals.

GENERAL

This fish is very common along the South African coast and through

out the Indo-Pacific region. Like the emperor angelfish the semicircle is well known to divers and is highly prized by marine aquarists, particularly in the juvenile form. It is very easy to approach and will seem to pose for the photographer.

OLD WOMAN

Ou vrou

Pomacanthus striatus (204.12)

DESCRIPTION (size: up to 50 cm)
Unlike the previous two related species the adult is quite drab. The overall body colour is brown, becoming lighter towards the tail. The juveniles are similar to those of the semicircle angelfish but the stripes are less pronounced.

HABITAT
This mid-water swimmer can be seen solitarily or in small numbers. The juveniles tend to inhabit rock pools close to the shore.

FEEDING HABITS
Feeds on plankton.

GENERAL
This is the most common of the *Pomacanthus* family and is found in the water columns off Sodwana Bay. It is often the first fish seen by a spearfisherman who drifts down-current towards a community of fish and as such is known as a "marker" fish.

THREADFIN BUTTERFLYFISH
Draadvin-vlindervis
Chaetodon auriga (205.1)

DESCRIPTION (size: up to 20 cm)
The body is white with thin black lines; the back and tail fin bright
yellow. There is a black spot, which looks like an eye, on the dorsal fin
and a wide black line runs vertically through the eye. The name is
derived from the thread-like filament extending from the soft dorsal
fin.

HABITAT
It inhabits coral and rocky reefs and is found swimming among the
coral heads. Like many of the hardier butterflyfish it can also be found
in rock pools close to the shore.

FEEDING HABITS
Carnivorous, eating worms and crustaceans.

GENERAL
It is fairly common off our coast and can easily be approached underwater.

GORGEOUS GUSSIE

Mooigussie

Chaetodon guttatissimus (205.6)

DESCRIPTION (size: up to 12 cm)
The body is beige with numerous black spots. A dark band runs vertically through the eye. The tail has yellow, black and translucent markings.

HABITAT
Seen either solitarily or in pairs in or just above the reef. It usually stays close to the coral into which it ducks when threatened.

FEEDING HABITS
It feeds on small invertebrates.

GENERAL
The gussie is a prized aquarium fish but is difficult to keep. Although one of the smaller butterflyfish it is quite easy to photograph.

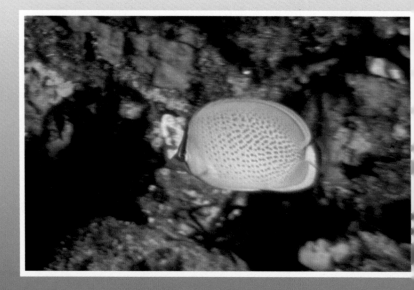

HALFMOON BUTTERFLYFISH
Halfmaan-vlindervis
Chaetodon lunula (205.9)

DESCRIPTION (size: up to 20 cm)
Sometimes called the racoon butterflyfish because of its face. Its general colour is yellow with a black band through the eye and a white band just above the eye.

HABITAT
Can be seen solitarily or in pairs in the more sheltered areas of the reef such as the underside of caves and coral heads as well as inshore rocky pools and gullies.

FEEDING HABITS
It feeds on coral polyps, molluscs, worms and fish eggs.

GENERAL
The adult is one of the largest butterflyfish and the most common off the South African coast. It is an active nocturnal feeder.

PEARLY BUTTERFLYFISH
Pêrel-vlindervis
Chaetodon madagaskariensis (205.10)

DESCRIPTION (size: up to 15 cm)
The body is pearly white with vertical arrowhead-shaped dark bands. The rear of the body and the tail fin are orange edged in white; the base of the tail is white. Its nose is more pointed than that of other butterflyfish.

HABITAT
It inhabits coral and rocky reefs and is often seen on the outer edges among the broken coral and rocks.

FEEDING HABITS
Feeds on small crustaceans and small amounts of seaweed.

GENERAL
In scientific terms it is sometimes incorrectly known as *C.chrysurus*. It is active at night and sleeps in crevasses during the day. It may cover large areas and roam from reef to reef.

DOUBLESASH BUTTERFLYFISH
Dubbelband-vlindervis
Chaetodon marleyi (205.11)

DESCRIPTION (size: up to 15 cm)
The *marleyi* is predominantly silvery white with two golden brown bands. The dorsal and anal fins are orange, pectoral fins are transparent. The tail is made up of silvery gold and transparent bands. The black spot, clearly visible on the adult, is absent on the juvenile.

HABITAT
Normally seen on the surface of the reef; here it is shown in its natural habitat on Limestone reef off Durban's Addington beach.

FEEDING HABITS
It feeds on both invertebrates and seaweed.

GENERAL
This unique photograph shows a feature of the defence mechanism of the butterflyfish. The black spot at the top of the second bar acts as a false eye, since the actual eye is camouflaged in the black bar at the sharp end of the fish. An attacker attempts to kill its prey by biting the eye, which turns out to be a false eye — hence the piece missing from the dorsal fin as in this case. The butterflyfish swims away from the

encounter minus a piece of its dorsal fin and with a dent in its dignity, but without losing its life.

The second photograph shows the whole fish, including the black spot towards the rear of its dorsal fin.

BLACKBACK BUTTERFLYFISH
Swartrug-vlindervis
Chaetodon melannotus (205.12)

DESCRIPTION (size: up to 15 cm)
The general body colour is white with thin black lines running at an angle across the body. The fins are bright yellow as are the nose and face. Towards the dorsal fin the colour becomes dark to black, hence the name.

HABITAT
Usually found in sheltered parts of the reef in areas of lush growth. Usually solitary but occasionally swims in pairs.

FEEDING HABITS
Feeds on sessile invertebrates.

GENERAL
This butterflyfish, common in the Red Sea, is seen in the Indian Ocean north of Mozambique. Not shy, it is easy to approach underwater.

MAYPOLE BUTTERFLYFISH
Meiboom-vlindervis
Chaetodon meyeri (205.13)

DESCRIPTION (size: up to 20 cm)
This is a beautiful little fish, body white with approximately eight black bands or stripes running at an angle through the body. The edges of the fins are yellow. It is easily identified as no other butterflyfish found in the Indian Ocean looks even vaguely similar. The body colour of the juvenile is blueish.

HABITAT
Found only on coral reefs, singly or in pairs, throughout the Indo-Pacific region.

FEEDING HABITS
Feeds on coral polyps.

GENERAL
It is very common off Sodwana Bay. Unlike most of the butterflyfish it is not easy to photograph, moving away from the diver when approached. It has a similar pattern to *C.ornatissimus* which is found on the Great Barrier Reef except that the bands are orange on the body and black on the face.

PURPLE BUTTERFLYFISH (STRIPED BUTTERFLYFISH)
Pers vlindervis
Chaetodon trifascialis (205.14)

DESCRIPTION (size: up to 20 cm)
This beautiful little butterflyfish looks similar to the blacktail butterflyfish but does not have the black tail. The background colour of the body is yellow with dark thin lines running horizontally, angled slightly upwards along the body. A dark band runs vertically through the eye. The bases of the dorsal and anal fins are dark and the caudal fin is black with white edging and a yellow base.

HABITAT
It can be seen swimming in the shallower reef areas, particularly among staghorn coral, as this picture shows.

FEEDING HABITS
It feeds on coral polyps.

GENERAL
This little fish can cover a wide area of the reef, taking little bites at the coral polyps along the way. It is not often seen off the South African coast.

LIMESPOT BUTTERFLYFISH
Eenkol-vlindervis
Chaetodon unimaculatus (205.16)

DESCRIPTION (size: up to 20 cm)
The background colour is uniformly bright yellow with a large black spot in the middle at the top of the body. The tail is translucent and a thick black line runs vertically through the eye.

HABITAT
This is a common coral reef resident and can be seen in pairs or small groups. It normally swims above the reef during the day.

FEEDING HABITS
It eats small crustaceans and soft corals.

GENERAL
The limespot is also known as the one-spot or teardrop. Like many of its genus it tends to flit like a butterfly from place to place. Its striking colours make it a favourite for photographers.

VAGABOND BUTTERFLYFISH
Swerwer-vlindervis
Chaetodon vagabundus (205.17)

DESCRIPTION (size: up to 20 cm)
The vagabond is not dissimilar to the blackback butterflyfish, but lacks the black back. The tail, rear of the body and dorsal fins are yellow. Two vertical black bands run through the base of the dorsal fin and the middle of the tail. There is also a black band running through the eye.

HABITAT
Normally found swimming in pairs close to the reef.

FEEDING HABITS
Its diet consists of small invertebrates, amphipods and worms.

GENERAL
The vagabond appears not to be territorial as pairs can be followed underwater for considerable distances. They are hardy and easy to keep in an aquarium.

BLACKTAIL BUTTERFLYFISH
Swartstert-vlindervis
Chaetodon austriacus

DESCRIPTION (size: up to 20 cm)
This very striking butterflyfish gets its name from the black dorsal and anal fins, distinctly seen in the picture. The background colour of the body is yellow, with thin black lines running longitudinally. The third line from the top thickens markedly near the back of the body. The face has vertical black and yellow bars running through it.

HABITAT
Usually seen in small groups swimming freely around the coral heads

FEEDING HABITS
It feeds on small invertebrates and algae.

GENERAL
This fish is rarely seen off the South African coast; it is common in the Red Sea and off the East African coast. It is easy to approach under water.

LONGNOSE BUTTERFLYFISH

Langneus-vlindervis

Forcipiger flavissimus (205.20)

DESCRIPTION (size: up to 16 cm)

This fish has a distinctive long nose, the upper half of which is dark brown, the lower half a light grey/white that ends at the base of the pectoral fin. The rest of the body is yellow with a black eye spot at the base of the tail. It can easily be mistaken for the other species of this genus, called *Forcipiger longirostris*; however, the dark brown colour in the latter ends at the eye.

HABITAT

Generally observed in pairs close to the surface of the reef. Swims upside down in caves.

FEEDING HABITS

Feeds on small invertebrates.

GENERAL

The very long nose or mouth, which can be likened to a pair of long-nosed pliers, is used for probing into holes for food species. It is not easy to approach underwater but when caught in the frame makes a beautiful model.

BRUSHTOOTH BUTTERFLYFISH
Borseltand-vlindervis
Hemitaurichthys zoster (205.21)

DESCRIPTION (size: up to 18 cm)
A dark brown to black fish with a wide white area in the middle of the body. The dorsal spines over the white area are yellow. By virtue of its black and white colours this fish could be called upon to represent Natal!

HABITAT
The brushtooth is normally seen in large shoals in the mid-water above the reef. Fairly large numbers can be seen at Two Mile, Nine Mile and the inshore reefs south of Mabibi.

FEEDING HABITS
It feeds on plankton found in the mid-water.

GENERAL
This hardy fish adapts well to aquarium conditions. Although free swimming the brushtooth is difficult to capture on film as it endeavours to keep out of photographic range.

COACHMAN

Koetsier

Heniochus acuminatus (205.22)

DESCRIPTION (size: up to 16 cm)
Colour mainly white with two wide black bands running vertically down the body; the pectoral, caudal and dorsal fins are yellow. It has a very long dorsal fin. This fish is often confused with the moorish idol which has much longer filaments and a more protruding mouth.

HABITAT
Found singly or in pairs both in the mid-water and just above the reef. Sometimes large numbers of semi-juveniles congregate, making a spectacular show of yellow, black and white.

FEEDING HABITS
It has a varied diet of mid-water plankton and small invertebrates.

GENERAL
This common resident can be seen all over the Sodwana area. It is easy to approach underwater and photograph. The coachman is often referred to as "the poor man's moorish idol".

MASKED COACHMAN

Gemaskerde koetsier

Heniochus monoceros (205.24)

DESCRIPTION (size: up to 24 cm)
Although similar in shape it can be distinguished from the coachman by the protuberance just above the eye and more yellow on the dorsal and anal fins.

HABITAT
Occasionally seen on the coral reefs; prefers the gullies and caves. It is rare in our area.

FEEDING HABITS
It feeds on small copepods and invertebrates.

GENERAL
The two specimens shown here were found on Two Mile Reef south of the north buoy in what is regarded as one of the most spectacular parts of this reef. These are the only two that the authors have seen on this coast.

MOZAMBIQUE KNIFEJAW (CUCKOO BASS)
Mosambiekse kraaibek
Oplegnathus peaolopesi (206.2)

DESCRIPTION (size: up to 70 cm)
The adult is a dark bronzy brown with a patch of yellow on the head. The overall colour tends to pale towards the rear. There is a distinct bump between the eyes.

HABITAT
This mid-water swimmer can also be seen feeding on the coral itself.

FEEDING HABITS
It is omnivorous and feeds on seaweed and sponges.

GENERAL
It is common off our coast and quite inquisitive. Although it has a similar beak to that of parrotfish, it is not related to them. This is one of the easiest fish in the sea to spear. It frequently swims up to a diver, turns sideways and waggles its pectoral fin as if indicating the place to put the spear. For the unwary spearfisherman it can produce a nasty bite from the sharp beak or a stab with the dorsal or anal spines. Divers regard these fish as the vermin of the sea.

YELLOWSPOTTED KINGFISH

Geelspikkel-koningvis

Carangoides fulvoguttatus (210.11)

DESCRIPTION (size: up to 100 cm)
This rather striking fish is blue/green above and silvery below. Adults often have three black blotches on the lateral line on the flanks. The fins have a yellowish tinge.

HABITAT
Mid-water swimmers, often seen in small shoals at the edge of the reef.

FEEDING HABITS
It feeds on small fish, mole crabs and sea lice. The "fulvie" is usually responsible for chasing shoals of bait fish in the early morning or late afternoon. It does not have strong jaws and hence chooses soft prey.

GENERAL
These fish are a favourite with spearfishermen and are frequently seen by divers in the mid-water off Sodwana Bay.

BLUEFIN KINGFISH
Blouvin-koningvis
Caranx melampygus (210.19)

DESCRIPTION (size: up to 80 cm)
Like many game fish, the bluefin appears to be silver. The overall colour is in fact a silvery green with more silver to white below. Many iridescent blue spots cover the top of the body. The fins have translucent tinges of blue at the edges. As in all kingfish a hard sharp bony tail extends laterally from the middle of the body.

HABITAT
Usually seen in small groups hunting just above the coral reefs.

FEEDING HABITS
Feeds on small shrimps and squid.

GENERAL
More frequently seen off our coast in the winter months than in summer. It is most active during the early hours of the morning and the late afternoon.

BLACKTIP KINGFISH
Swarttip-koningvis
Caranx sem (210.21)

DESCRIPTION (size: up to 100 cm)
A popular game fish, the blacktip is dark bronze to yellow-green above and more silvery bronze to yellowish below. The tail is yellow below and white above with a distinctive black tip. The dorsal and anal fins are bright yellow.

HABITAT
It prefers clean water and can be seen in small groups over deep rocky reefs.

FEEDING HABITS
Feeds on small fish, shrimps and crabs.

GENERAL
It is seen more frequently in the summer months than in winter. Large shoals can be found on the deep reefs off Durban's Bluff and the Natal south coast. Popular with spearfishermen.

GIANT YELLOWTAIL

Reuse geelstert

Seriola lalandi (210.44)

DESCRIPTION (size: up to 150 cm)
The blue-green upper body is separated from silvery flanks by a broad yellow-bronze band which runs the entire length of the body. The belly is white and the fins yellow.

HABITAT
Normally found in large shoals swimming in the mid-water or close to the surface.

FEEDING HABITS
It feeds on small fish, occasionally shrimps and crabs.

GENERAL
Although it can grow to 150 cm and 50 kg those in the picture are closer to 20 kg. Large shoals of yellowtail frequently follow the sardine run up the Natal coast. It makes excellent eating and is one of the most exciting game fish for fishermen and spearfishermen alike. It is relatively easy to approach underwater and seeing one is a great thrill to divers.

PRODIGAL SON

Kobia

Rachycentron canadum (212.1)

DESCRIPTION (size: up to 2 m)
Overall dark brownish with a silvery band running longitudinally.

HABITAT
This mid-water swimmer is often seen with other large fish such as whale sharks, other sharks and, as the picture shows, rays.

FEEDING HABITS
It feeds mainly on crustaceans.

GENERAL
This is a great fighting fish and makes excellent eating. Nearly all have parasitic worms in the stomach but these do not appear to have any adverse effects on their host. When seen in murky water, particularly when approaching head on, the prodigal is often mistaken for a shark and as it is an inquisitive fish that may swim right up to a diver, this can be an unnerving misidentification. Fishermen report that if a prodigal son is landed, there is often a good chance that a second one will be caught. This gives weight to the observations of divers who have seen prodigal sons following hooked mates into shallow water, almost to the shore.

FRECKLED HAWKFISH

Gesproete valkvis

Paracirrhites forsteri (214.7)

DESCRIPTION (size: up to 25 cm)
The body is light brown with two distinct whitish-yellow lines, one along the lateral line and the other along the dorsal fin. The face is light grey with dark speckles that extend to the pectoral fins.

HABITAT
Normally seen alone sitting on plate or branching coral, as shown in the picture.

FEEDING HABITS
Carnivorous, eating crustaceans.

GENERAL
It is common in our waters and because it tends to sit and look around it is easy to approach underwater. It makes an ideal aquarium fish.

FOURBAR DAMSEL
Vierbalk-nooientjie
Abudefduf natalensis (219.1)

DESCRIPTION (size: up to 17 cm)

There are approximately 300 species of damselfish, of which some 45 species of 12 genera are found off the South African coast. This is one of the most common, having a light grey body with four distinct vertical bars. The fourth runs through the base of the tail. The dorsal fins are edged in blue.

HABITAT

Most abundant on coral reefs, seen singly or in shoals of up to several hundred fish.

FEEDING HABITS

Feeds on small crustaceans, plankton and algae.

GENERAL

This is quite a cheeky fish and may actually attempt to bite divers, particularly on exposed parts such as ankles or wrists.

TWOBAR ANEMONEFISH

Tweebalk-anemoonvis

Amphiprion allardi (219.9)

DESCRIPTION (size: up to 14 cm)
This cute little fish, commonly known to divers as the clownfish, is generally dark brown with the ventral regions yellow. All fins except the paler caudal fin are bright yellow. Two tapering white vertical stripes divide the fish into thirds, giving it a clown-like appearance.

HABITAT
Very common, living in symbiosis with sea anemones (usually the long tentacled species: *Hetarctis* and *Stichodactyla*). Pairs are found swimming in the anemone's tentacles.

FEEDING HABITS
Eats small marine worms, algae and crustaceans that are attracted by the anemone.

GENERAL
The anemone's tentacles are poisonous but the twobar is immune to this poison. This fish is extremely aggressive in protecting its territory and will attack and bite divers who encroach — very comical for a fish its size. It is easily bred in captivity; the first successful attempts to do this were achieved in South Africa. It lays eggs in clusters on a rock

near the anemone and spends hours fanning them until the eggs hatch. Usually a pair is found with each anemone, although where anemones are in short supply, two or more pairs may share a home. One of the reasons for the successful breeding of twobars may be the feasibility of capturing a pair.

The second picture shows a single twobar, taken in the Red Sea near Eliat, which seems to indicate that the twobar is more widespread than either the Smiths or Rudi van Elst would suggest.

DOMINO

Domino

Dascyllus trimaculatus (219.27)

DESCRIPTION (size: up to 14 cm)
The body is black or very dark brown with three spots, one on either flank and one on the forehead. The latter fades with age and the spots on the flanks get smaller.

HABITAT
Very common on coral reefs, frequently associating with sea urchins. Can be seen singly or in small shoals.

FEEDING HABITS
Feeds on invertebrates and small fish.

GENERAL
This common reef inhabitant is easy to approach underwater. It is preyed upon by some of the larger reef fish. The photograph shows a large shoal feeding on dead fish.

LYRETAIL HOGFISH

Lierstert-varkvis

Bodianus anthioides (220.5)

DESCRIPTION (size: up to 20 cm)
The front of the body to just before the anal fin is a rusty orange.
brown; the rest of the body is white with brown speckles. The upper
and lower extremities of the caudal fin are edged in brown, which
extends to the anal base. As with most wrasses colour variations occur
between juveniles and adults.

HABITAT
A resident of coral reefs but not common in our waters.

FEEDING HABITS
It feeds on small fish, crustaceans and molluscs.

GENERAL
This is not an easy fish to identify because of the colour variations. In
addition it is difficult to photograph as it usually presents the pho
tographer with a tail view.

TURNCOAT HOGFISH

Weerhaan-varkvis

Bodianus axillaris (220.6)

DESCRIPTION (size: up to 20 cm)
The juvenile has a black body with approximately 12 white spots evenly distributed over it, as shown in the picture. It has a translucent caudal fin. The adult is reddish brown in front and white behind with a black dot at the base of the anal fin.

HABITAT
Adults are seen swimming around the reef, juveniles are more likely to hide in caves.

FEEDING HABITS
Carnivorous, feeding on crustaceans.

GENERAL
It is territorial and can be seen to follow regular swimming patterns around its base area. In Australia it is known as the axil pigfish. The juveniles make excellent aquarium fish but prefer some dark places in which to shelter.

SADDLEBACK HOGFISH
Saalrug-varkvis
Bodianus bilunulatus (220.7)

DESCRIPTION (size: up to 60 cm)
Colour a general reddish brown with a paler yellow/white belly. There are definite yellow markings along the upper caudal fin. The most prominent feature is the large "saddle" marking just behind the dorsal fin. Changes and variations in coloration occur.

HABITAT
Found in and around deep coral and rocky reefs.

FEEDING HABITS
It feeds on gastropods, limpets, sea urchins and crabs. Prey is crushed by grinding plates in the mouth.

GENERAL
Like many wrasses it moves with an undulating motion and is seldom stationary, making photography difficult.

DIANA'S HOGFISH
Diana se varkvis
Bodianus diana (220.8)

DESCRIPTION (size: up to 25 cm)
This striking little fish is a bronzy colour with the upper-body scales edged in black. There is a black spot in the middle of the tail and four to six yellow/golden spots along the upper flanks between the dorsal fin and the lateral line. The juvenile is black with white spots and looks similar to the turncoat hogfish. The only difference is that Diana's has no white nose.

HABITAT
A solitary fish that can be seen along the faces of rocky and coral reefs.

FEEDING HABITS
Eats any hard-shelled organisms.

GENERAL
Shy and not easily approached underwater. The juveniles spend most of their time in caves, like turncoat juveniles.

QUEEN CORIS

Koningin-coris

Coris formosa (220.22)

DESCRIPTION (size: up to 60 cm)
The photograph shows an adult: the head and body are green/brown with two green stripes running behind the eye. The anal fin is edged in blue and the caudal fin is red and blue. The juvenile is totally different, being dark brown with a wide vertical white band crossing the body and dorsal fin.

HABITAT
Found swimming around coral reefs.

FEEDING HABITS
A bottom feeder that eats small marine animals.

GENERAL
This is a spectacular fish but its darting movements make it particularly difficult to photograph. Extremely popular with marine aquarists, especially in the juvenile form.

AFRICAN CORIS

Afrikaanse coris

Coris gaimard africana (220.23)

DESCRIPTION (size: up to 35 cm)
The juvenile, pictured here, is very similar to the queen coris juvenile. The difference is that the white bands in the African coris are shorter. Adults are a brown/violet colour with many blue spots; they have blue markings on the face and the tail is yellow. Males develop a light green vertical bar on the body.

HABITAT
Found swimming along the surface of the reef.

FEEDING HABITS
Feeds on small living marine animals.

GENERAL
Extremely popular with marine aquarists, particularly in the juvenile form.

CHECKERBOARD WRASSE
Geruite lipvis
Halichoeres hortulanus (220.30)

DESCRIPTION (size: up to 26 cm)
The juvenile is very mottled. The adult, as shown in the photograph, has white squares edged in black with a large spot just behind the dorsal fin. The tail fin, dorsal and caudal fins are yellow and the head greenish with pink bands.

HABITAT
A reef dweller, usually seen alone.

FEEDING HABITS
It feeds on a variety of small invertebrates.

GENERAL
It is rather skittish and being a fast swimmer is not easy to photograph. Although seen at Sodwana, it is not very common.

RINGED WRASSE

Geringde lipvis

Hologymnosus doliatus (220.38)

DESCRIPTION (size: up to 38 cm)
The juvenile is white with three orange-red stripes. The adult is light blue-green with lavender blue bars. A pale zone in the pectoral region is bordered by vertical purple bands. The head is blue-green with irregular orange bands; the tail has similar markings.

HABITAT
Usually seen in and around coral reefs.

FEEDING HABITS
It feeds on small fish and crustaceans.

GENERAL
The patterns on this fish give it the appearance of an X-ray photograph: it looks rather like a skeleton.

GOLDBAR WRASSE
Goudstaaf-lipvis
Thalassoma hebraicum (220.61)

DESCRIPTION (size: up to 23 cm)
Easily identified by the bright yellow bar running vertically just behind the pectoral fin. The juvenile is very different, being blackish with two staggered longitudinal rows of large diffused yellow spots and a yellow bar from the base of the dorsal spine running behind the pectoral fin to the belly.

HABITAT
Very common, seen swimming in and among the coral.

FEEDING HABITS
It eats mainly corals, molluscs and sea urchins which it breaks up with its strong teeth and then crushes. The shell parts are then ejected through the gills.

GENERAL
The male is fiercely territorial and may keep up to half a dozen females at any one time. As with sea goldies sex reversal takes place.

CRESCENT-TAIL WRASSE

Maanstert-lipvis

Thalassoma lunare (220.62)

DESCRIPTION (size: up to 25 cm)
The overall head and body colour is green, the head covered with ir-regular purple lines. There is a purple blotch in the centre of the pec-toral fin and the caudal fin is yellow edged in blue and purple. The anal and dorsal fins are purple with blue outlines.

HABITAT
Often found swimming in groups along the surface of the reef.

FEEDING HABITS
Eats mainly invertebrates and small fish.

GENERAL
This beautiful wrasse is common in the Sodwana Bay area. It is fairly easy to approach and photograph.

EMBER PARROTFISH
Kool-papegaaivis
Scarus rubroviolaceus (221.15)

DESCRIPTION (size: up to 66 cm)
This prolific inhabitant of Sodwana is predominantly blue with a yellowish hue in the mid-lateral line. However, great colour variations can occur as the two pictures show. The parrot-like beak is used to crush coral.

HABITAT
It likes rich coral growth areas and can be seen swimming just above the surface of the reef.

FEEDING HABITS
In crushing the coral it feeds on algae and is known as a reef grazer.

GENERAL
It makes good eating but is protected from spearfishing because like the cuckoo bass it is very easy to shoot. Because of the parrot-like beak and eating habits it is not often caught by anglers.

There is concern that in some coral areas of the world the parrotfish is responsible for overgrazing and hence destroying the coral faster than it can be replaced. In this it is likened to the crown of thorns star-fish, which is a problem on some coral reefs.

BLACKFIN BARRACUDA
Swartvin-barrakuda
Sphyraena qenie (224.10)

DESCRIPTION (size: up to 115 cm)
This sleek silver gamefish has 18-22 dark crossbars running vertically to well below the lateral line. These bars tend to be broken in the middle. The dorsal and caudal fins are dark with black edging.

HABITAT
A migratory mid-water swimmer, usually found in large shoals.

FEEDING HABITS
It feeds on small fish and squid.

GENERAL
Often confused with the pickhandle barracuda (*S.jello*) or the sawtooth barracuda (*S.putnamiae*). The only easy way to tell them apart is that the crossbars on *S. jello* and *S. putnamiae* do not extend as far below the lateral line as those of *S. qenie*. *S. jello* has 20 vertical bars and *S. putnamiae* has 15, but it is unlikely that the diver will be given an opportunity to make an accurate count under the water. It is easy to spear as the large shoals tend to wheel around the diver. The photograph is unusual as the lighting effect was produced by a 12-volt sealed beam car headlight.

PENCILLED SURGEON
Potlood-doktervis
Acanthurus dussumieri (243.2)

DESCRIPTION (size: up to 55 cm)
Identified by the yellow band that extends forward from the eye. There is also yellow behind the eye. The caudal fin is blue with numerous black spots and a white base. The caudal spine sheath is white. The dorsal fin is yellow and the anal fin olive, edged in white.

HABITAT
Found singly, swimming in the reef.

FEEDING HABITS
Herbivorous, eating algae.

GENERAL
Like all surgeonfish it has very sharp caudal spines, which are extended when the fish is threatened. Care must therefore be taken when handling any surgeonfish.

POWDER-BLUE SURGEONFISH

Poeierblou-doktervis

Acanthurus leucosternon (243.3)

DESCRIPTION (size: up to 23 cm)
This lovely-looking fish is a great favourite of divers. It has a blue
body, black face and a white band between the underside of the jaw
and the pectoral fin. The dorsal fin is yellow with white edging, the
anal fin and pelvic fins are white and the caudal fin is white edged in
black.

HABITAT
Found around coral bombies, normally in the shallower areas, usually
in groups of up to six, but spectacular shoals of up to 50 can be seen.

FEEDING HABITS
It eats algae and occasionally crustaceans.

GENERAL
A very easy fish to photograph, it is often called the painted surgeon as
it tends to pose for its portrait.

BLUEBANDED SURGEON
Blouband-doktervis
Acanthurus lineatus (243.4)

DESCRIPTION (size: up to 38 cm)
The whole body is covered with alternating black-lined blue and yellow stripes. The belly is powder blue, the fins are grey outlined in iridescent blue.

HABITAT
It normally lives on the perimeter of the reef where it is exposed to water motion.

FEEDING HABITS
It feeds on algae.

GENERAL
A large school of bluebanded surgeon, with many surgeonfish, can often be seen on the reef close to shore about 1 km south of Mabibi point. The blades on the caudal fin are razor sharp and poisonous.

LIEUTENANT SURGEONFISH

Luitenant-doktervis

Acanthurus tennenti (243.9)

DESCRIPTION (size: up to 31 cm)
The juvenile is brown with a horseshoe-shaped black mark opening forwards on the shoulder region. In fish longer than 12 cm this mark breaks into two black bands pointing backwards, as seen in the picture. The overall body colour is grey with the fins outlined in black or blue.

HABITAT
It is rare in our area and may only be seen around coral heads.

FEEDING HABITS
Herbivorous, eating algae.

GENERAL
The authors have only seen two or three off our coast, so taking this photograph was very good fortune.

SPOTTED BRISTLETOOTH
Gespikkelde borseltand
Ctenochaetus strigosus (243.15)

DESCRIPTION (size: up to 18 cm)
Brown overall with a yellow semi-circle around the eye. The pectoral fin is yellow.

HABITAT
Seen individually or in pairs around the coral heads, but not common.

FEEDING HABITS
It eats algae.

GENERAL
The caudal spine, once thought to be venomous, was later found not to be so. The fish occurs all over the world; there are considerable variations in colour from ocean to ocean. Little more is known about this fish.

SAILFIN TANG

Seilvin-tang

Zebrasoma veliferum (243.19)

DESCRIPTION (size: up to 40 cm)
Dark olive-brown with yellow spots on the lower body. Narrow yellow bands, broader towards the head, run vertically down the body. The face is white with little black spots. The dorsal and anal fins have broadly curving, alternating dark brown and yellow bands.

HABITAT
It is not common but may be found in the sheltered areas of the reef.

FEEDING HABITS
It feeds on filamentous algae.

GENERAL
This fish is spectacular if seen with the fins fully extended as shown in the picture.

PURPLE SURGEON
Pers doktervis
Zebrasoma xanthurus

DESCRIPTION (size: up to 50 cm)
This unbelievable-looking surgeon is purple with a bright yellow tail
and a yellow margin on the pectoral fin. There are two yellow dots
between the eyes.

HABITAT
Has been sighted north of Madagascar swimming around shallow
coral heads.

FEEDING HABITS
Feeds on algae.

GENERAL
This fish is very common in the Red Sea and can be easily approached
underwater. No diver will ever forget a sighting of this beautiful fish,
shown here swimming with a school of sea goldies.

ORANGE-SPINE UNICORN
Oranje stekel-eenhoringvis
Naso lituratus (243.25)

DESCRIPTION (size: up to 45 cm)
The body is an olive-greenish grey colour with a yellow forehead. The caudal peduncle has a pair of thorn-like projections. The male has a long filament on the top and bottom of the tail.

HABITAT
Fairly common, found very close to the reef.

FEEDING HABITS
It feeds on algae.

GENERAL
Although common it is not easy to approach underwater and retreats into caves or crevasses if harassed. It is particularly difficult to photograph, always presenting an end-on view. It seldom extends its dorsal and anal fins while swimming.

MOORISH IDOL
Moorse afgod
Zanclus canescens (Z. cornutus) (244.1)

DESCRIPTION (size: up to 22 cm)
Related to the surgeonfish but lacking the blades on the caudal fin. It has black and yellow broad bands and the upper dorsal has a long white filament. It is occasionally confused with the coachman, the latter however does not have the protruding mouth.

HABITAT
Seen alone or in small groups, occasionally in large numbers. This is thought to be a prelude to spawning.

FEEDING HABITS
It feeds on small sponges.

GENERAL
A graceful swimmer and fairly easy to approach underwater although it seldom stops swimming. At night it adopts a totally different coloration; the broad yellow band becomes dark, making the fish very difficult to see.

CLOWN TRIGGERFISH (WAISTCOAT TRIGGERFISH)

Nar-snellervis

Balistoides conspicillum (263.4)

DESCRIPTION (size: up to 50 cm)
Very striking: the body is black with large white spots covering the lower half. It has orange "clown" lips and a yellow bar over the bridge of the nose. The scales around the dorsal fin are edged in yellow.

HABITAT
A mid-water swimmer common over the entire Indo-Pacific region.

FEEDING HABITS
It feeds on sea urchins and crustaceans.

GENERAL
A popular yet very expensive aquarium fish. It is not easy to get close to underwater, but divers often hear it grunt. Like most triggerfish it will hide in a cave if chased, where it will extend its dorsal spine to lock itself into position, making it very difficult to remove. When this dorsal spine is locked it cannot be folded down unless the second dorsal spine or "trigger" is depressed, hence the name triggerfish.

DOTTY TRIGGERFISH

Gestippelde snellervis

Balistoides viridescens (263.5)

DESCRIPTION (size: up to 70 cm)
Quite a plump fish that can be considered ugly. The face and the base of the tail are pale. The main body appears black with a yellow wire mesh pattern.

HABITAT
Usually seen in and around the coral reefs.

FEEDING HABITS
Not known.

GENERAL
Rarely seen by divers; however, one has been known to live close to the north buoy on Two Mile Reef at Sodwana. More information is needed on this fish, particularly pertaining to its feeding habits and juveniles.

INDIAN TRIGGERFISH
Indiese snellervis
Melichthys indicus (263.7)

DESCRIPTION (size: up to 25 cm)
The body is dark to black with a narrow white margin around the caudal, anal and dorsal fins.

HABITAT
Normally seen swimming face down feeding off the coral.

FEEDING HABITS
It feeds on algae and zooplankton.

GENERAL
Shy and not easily approached, darting away quickly; consequently quite difficult to photograph.

BLACK TRIGGERFISH

Swart snellervis

Melichthys niger (263.8)

DESCRIPTION (size: up to 35 cm)
Blueish overall with a softer blue line along the base of the dorsal and caudal fins.

HABITAT
Large numbers can be seen in the mid-water on the up-current side of the reef.

FEEDING HABITS
Its diet consists of calcareous algae and zooplankton.

GENERAL
A shy fish and not easily approached. If it is near the coral it will dart into an opening whenever it feels threatened in any way, making photography difficult.

HALFMOON TRIGGERFISH
Halfmaan-snellervis
Sufflamen chrysopterus (263.16)

DESCRIPTION (size: up to 30 cm)
A brown fish; the yellow caudal fin has white margins. There is a white stripe running downwards from just below the eye.

HABITAT
Normally seen in the sheltered areas of the reef.

FEEDING HABITS
It feeds on algae and zooplankton.

GENERAL
This very shy fish always has escape holes nearby. When retreating into one of these it bites onto the coral and jams itself in by extending its dorsal fin. At this stage nothing short of demolishing the coral head will remove it.

BOXY

Koffertjie

Ostracion cubicus (266.6)

DESCRIPTION [size: up to 45 cm]
The adult male is a brilliant yellow with blue dorsal surfaces; the female is basically olive. The juvenile is bright yellow with large black spots.

HABITAT
Usually seen swimming in the mid-water, although juveniles tend to remain in caves. It can also be seen in rock pools close to the shore.

FEEDING HABITS
Omnivorous.

GENERAL
The juvenile fish looks like a brightly coloured pea and is almost cubic in shape. Although rather slow moving, since it uses its side fins to swim with, it is highly manoeuvrable. It makes an excellent aquarium fish.

WHITESPOTTED BOXFISH
Witspikkel-koffervis
Ostracion meleagris (266.7)

DESCRIPTION (size: up to 25 cm)
Juveniles and females are blue or green with white spots. The adult male has orange bands with white spots on the upper body; the sides and belly are blue-grey, covered in red spots. The translucent fins are also covered in spots. Both colorations are featured in the photographs. This fish is referred to in some scientific works as *O. lentiginosus* or *O. lentiginosum.*

HABITAT
Found swimming in and around the reefs.

FEEDING HABITS
Feeds on sessile invertebrates, sponges and algae.

GENERAL
Slow moving and easy to approach underwater. When harassed it releases a toxic substance into the water. The flesh is poisonous.

The whitespotted boxfish is popular with marine aquarists as it happily coexists with other species and can be fed on brineshrimp or Daphnia.

MAP BLAASOP (PUFFER)

Kaart-blaasop

Arothron mappa (268.5)

DESCRIPTION (size: up to 55 cm)
This is the largest of the blaasop family. It is heavily built with beautiful markings: a maze of black lines on a beige body.

HABITAT
Inhabits coral reefs but is not common off our coast.

FEEDING HABITS
Feeds on algae and molluscs.

GENERAL
The photograph is of a very large adult that could easily have been larger than the maximum size stated above. It is easy to approach underwater. The flesh is deadly poisonous.

The name Blaasop is only found in South African publications. In most other parts of the world the genus arothron are refered to as Pufferfish.

GUINEAFOWL BLAASOP (PUFFER)

Tarentaal-blaasop

Arothron meleagris (268.6)

DESCRIPTION (size: up to 35 cm)
The body is brown/grey, densely covered with white spots. It is very similar to the whitespotted boxfish but the guineafowl's white spots are denser.

HABITAT
Found around the coral reefs.

FEEDING HABITS
Omnivorous.

GENERAL
Photographed at the bottom edge of the coral at Nine Mile Reef. It is slow moving and easy to photograph.

BLACKSPOTTED BLAASOP (PUFFER)

Swartspikkel-blaasop

Arothron nigropunctatus (268.7)

DESCRIPTION (size: up to 30 cm)
The body is yellow, sparsely covered with black spots. A wide variety
of colours can occur; the variation depicted here is possibly the most
beautiful.

HABITAT
Fairly common, it swims close to the reef.

FEEDING HABITS
It is a scavenger and will eat almost anything.

GENERAL
Slow swimming and very easy to approach and photograph.

YELLOW-SPOTTED BURRFISH (SPINY GLOBEFISH)
Geelspikkel-klitsvis
Cyclichthys spilostylus (C. echinatus) (269.3)

DESCRIPTION (size: up to 28 cm)
The body is basically white and is covered with many black-based spines. The dorsal area is yellow.

HABITAT
Seen swimming both in the mid-water and close to the surface of the reef.

FEEDING HABITS
It feeds on hard-shelled invertebrates.

GENERAL
This is quite a friendly fish and can be stroked by divers, at which time it will puff itself up to twice its normal size, as is clearly shown in the photograph.

GLOSSARY OF TERMS

amphipod:	a small crustacean lacking a rigid shell
anal fin:	the fin just below the tail
anterior:	the front of the fish
bivalves:	molluscs with two shells, such as oysters
caudal blades:	the sharp blades at the base of the tail on surgeonfish
caudal fin:	the tail fin
caudal peduncle:	the area where the tail fin attaches to the body
cephalopods:	a class of mollusc to which squid and octopus belong
ciguatera:	a fish toxin poisonous to man
compressed:	the body of the fish is flattened looking at it from the top
copepods:	very small crustaceans, most of which are free swimming
coral bombie:	a large head of coral
coral polyps:	the tiny animals that are continually building the coral with hard secretions
crustaceans:	invertebrate animals such as crayfish, crabs and prawns
dorsal fin:	the fin on the back of the fish
gamefish:	so called for their fighting qualities
gill:	the respiratory organ of a fish
gill rakers:	the appendages in the gill that filter food from water passing through the gill
invertebrate:	an animal without a backbone
lateral line:	the line that runs lengthwise along the side of the fish
mid-water:	the area between the surface of the water and the sea-bed
mollusc:	an invertebrate usually with an outer shell, such as mussels
pectoral fin:	the fin attached to the chest of the fish

pelagic:	describes fish that swim around freely in the open sea
plankton:	microscopic animal and plant organisms, including the larval forms of many invertebrates, suspended in the water
posterior:	the rear of the fish
rakers:	see gill rakers
salpas:	transparent planktonic animals
spiracles:	respiratory openings behind the eyes
symbiosis:	a relationship between different animals where both parties benefit
water column:	a body of water that extends from the surface to the sea bed
zooplankton :	the animal component of plankton

FISH CHECKLIST BY FAMILY

Whale sharks (*Rhincodontidae*)
  Whale shark

Ragged-tooth sharks
  (*Odontaspididae*)
  Spotted ragged-tooth

Eaglerays (*Myliobatidae*)
  Spotted eagleray

Stingrays (*Dasyatidae*)
  Honeycomb stingray
  Round ribbontailray

Moray eels (*Muraenidae*)
  Honeycomb moray

Pineapple fishes
  (*Monocentridae*)
  Pineapple fish

Soldierfishes (*Myripristinae*)
  Blotcheye soldier
  Deepwater soldier (horned
  squirrelfish)

Trumpetfishes (*Aulostomidae*)
  Trumpetfish

Flutemouths (*Fistulariidae*)
  Smooth flutemouth

Shrimpfishes (*Centriscidae*)
  Shrimpfish (razor fish)

Scorpionfishes (*Scorpaenidae*)
  Devil firefish
  Raggy scorpionfish
  Stonefish

Rockcods and seabasses
  (*Serranidae*)

Sea goldie (orange fairy
basslet)
Coral rockcod
Catface rockcod
Brownspotted rockcod
Redbarred rockcod
Yellowtail rockcod
Yellowbelly rockcod
Potato bass
Yellow-edge lyretail (swallow-
tail rockcod)

Soapfishes (*Grammistidae*)
  Sixstripe soapfish

Dottybacks (*Pseudochromidae*)
  Dutoiti

Bigeyes (*Priacanthidae*)
  Glass bigeye
  Crescent-tail bigeye

Rubberlips and grunters
  (*Haemulidae*)
  Lemonfish
  Whitebarred rubberlip
  Minstrel (grey sweetlips)

Snappers (*Lutjanidae*)
  River snapper (rock salmon)
  Bluebanded snapper
  Humpback snapper (paddle-
  tail)

Fusiliers (*Caesionidae*)
  Blue-and-gold fusilier
  Beautiful fusilier

Seabreams (*Sparidae*)
  Englishman

Wildeperd (zebra)
Cape stumpnose
Natal stumpnose

Emperors (*Lethrinidae*)
Blue emperor

Batfish (*Ephippidae*)
Longfin batfish
Spadefish

Goatfishes (*Mullidae*)
Two-saddle goatfish

Kobs (*Sciaenidae*)
Kob (kabeljou)
Baardman (tasselfish)

Angelfishes (*Pomacanthidae*)
Threespot angelfish
Emperor angelfish
Semicircle angelfish
Old woman

Butterflyfishes (*Chaetodontidae*)
Threadfin butterflyfish
Gorgeous gussie
Halfmoon butterflyfish
Pearly butterflyfish
Doublesash butterflyfish
Blackback butterflyfish
Maypole butterflyfish
Purple butterflyfish (striped butterflyfish)
Limespot butterflyfish
Vagabond butterflyfish
Blacktail butterflyfish
Longnose butterflyfish
Brushtooth butterflyfish
Coachman
Masked coachman

Knifejaws (*Oplegnathidae*)
Mozambique knifejaw (cuckoo bass)

Kingfishes (*Carangidae*)
Yellowspotted kingfish
Bluefin kingfish
Blacktip kingfish
Giant yellowtail

Cobia (*Rachycentridae*)
Prodigal son

Hawkfishes (*Cirrhitidae*)
Freckled hawkfish

Damselfishes (*Pomacentridae*)
Fourbar damsel
Twobar anemonefish
Domino

Wrasses (*Labridae*)
Lyretail hogfish
Turncoat hogfish
Saddleback hogfish
Diana's hogfish
Queen coris
African coris
Checkerboard wrasse
Ringed wrasse
Goldbar wrasse
Crescent-tail wrasse

Parrotfishes (*Scaridae*)
Ember parrotfish

Barracudas (*Sphyraenidae*)
Blackfin barracuda

Surgeonfishes and unicornfishes (*Acanthuridae*)
Pencilled surgeon
Powder-blue surgeonfish
Bluebanded surgeon
Lieutenant surgeonfish
Spotted bristletooth
Sailfin tang
Purple surgeon
Orange-spine unicorn

Moorish idol (*Zanclidae*)
  Moorish idol

Triggerfishes (*Balistidae*)
  Clown triggerfish (waistcoat triggerfish)
  Dotty triggerfish
  Indian triggerfish
  Black triggerfish
  Halfmoon triggerfish

Boxfishes (*Ostraciidae*)
  Boxy
  Whitespotted boxfish

Blaasops or puffers (*Tetraodontidae*)
  Map blaasop (puffer)
  Guineafowl blaasop (puffer)
  Blackspotted blaasop (puffer)

Burrfishes and porcupinefishes (*Diodontidae*)
  Yellow-spotted burrfish (spiny globefish)

BIBLIOGRAPHY

Buchsbaum, Ralph. *Animals without Backbones* Vol 1 & 2. Great Britain. Penguin Books. 1972.

Cohen, Shlomo. *Red Sea Divers Guide.* Tel Aviv. Seapen Books. 1988.

Coleman, Neville. *Australian Sea Fishes North of 30 Degrees South.* Sydney. Doubleday Australia. 1981.

Compagno, L.J.V., D.A. Ebert and M.J. Smale, *Guide to the Sharks and Rays of Southern Africa.* Cape Town. Struik Publishers. 1989.

Mills, Dick. *The Practical Encyclopedia of the Marine Aquarium.* London. Salamander Books. 1987.

Reader's Digest Book of the Great Barrier Reef. London. Reader's Digest Services. 1984.

Smith, Margaret M. and Phillip C. Heemstra. *Smiths' Sea Fishes.* Johannesburg. Southern Book Publishers. 1988.

Van der Elst, Rudy. *A Guide to the Common Sea Fishes of Southern Africa.* Cape Town. C. Struik. 1981.

Van der Elst, Rudy and Roy Vermeulen. *Sharks and Stingrays.* Cape Town. C. Struik. 1986.

148

INDEX TO SPECIES

INDEX TO AFRIKAANS COMMON NAMES